Rituals for Women Coping with Breast Cancer

The Prism Collective

Rituals for Women Coping with Breast Cancer

Copyright © 2000 by The Prism Collective

All Rights Reserved

Publisher's Cataloging-in-Publication
(Provided by Quality Books, Inc.)

Rituals for women coping with breast cancer / Rosalie
Muschal-Reinhardt ... [et al.]. -- 1st ed.
p. cm.
ISBN: 1-890662-10-0

1. Breast--Cancer--Patients--Religious life.
2. Spiritual healing. 3. Ritual. 4. Self-help
groups.   I. Muschal-Reinhardt, Rosalie.

BL619.H43R58 2000   291.4'42
                            QBI99-1971

Manufactured in Rochester, NY, USA

Cover and Book Design by Bash! Studios

These rituals are dedicated to all women
who are touched by breast cancer...

To those who experience the disease...

To those who care for them both
physically and spiritually...

And to those who love them.

Table of Contents

An Introduction

Today, one in eight women will develop breast cancer and face coping with its terrors. At the same time, she must make reasonable choices for health and maintain personal, family and professional relationships as well. Several years ago, The Prism Collective, a group of writers concerned with the spiritual needs of women, gathered together a collection of rituals marking significant moments in women's lives that are often trivialized or forgotten. Upon the publication of *Sisters of the Thirteen Moons*, we discovered that women are hungry to express and interpret their experiences in ways that move them beyond the rational and into the realm of the spiritual.

The rituals collected here are an outgrowth of our work with and awareness of the needs and wants of women who have experienced the many physical and emotional difficulties of breast cancer.

In listening to women who have breast cancer, we found that many of them experience similar emotions. The fears that accompany cancer often follow patterns, and, while the particulars may differ, they all need and long for support as they look for ways to articulate their fears and feelings.

In speaking with women who have breast cancer, we discovered that there is little in the way of spiritual nourishment for them as they face the arduousness of such a journey. In response to their promptings, we created this series of rituals designed to mark some of these common experiences.

Once touched by this disease, a woman and those who love her, can never look at life in quite the same way as they did before. For all of them, the lens has been refocused unalterably. These rituals suggest ways of creating moments that recognize the spiritual needs evoked by the vision through this new lens. The experience of breast cancer forces them to ask the most basic spiritual questions: Who am I as a woman with breast cancer? How does the loss of a breast affect my self-esteem? How can I cope with the conflicting emotions of hope and fear? How do I believe in myself and my ability to heal? How do I learn to place my trust in strangers?

They call together communities of caring people whose lives are interconnected because one of them has been diagnosed with a life-threatening disease. Because of the organic nature of ritual, that meaning grows out of interconnectedness, each community will manifest itself uniquely, expressing the spirit of those participating. We encourage you to pay attention to that spirit; follow some of our ideas, incorporate others, change the order, the method, substitute a different symbol—make them your own.

The rituals included here address five phases of dealing with breast cancer:

- *Acknowledging that one has breast cancer;*
- *Having confidence that one has made sound choices regarding treatment;*
- *Coping with the myriad emotions that accompany breast cancer and its treatment;*
- *Naming fears and losses and grieving for them;*
- *Celebrating hope for a healthy future.*

In the Greek myths, the story of Pandora's Box is one that is of interest to us. We use it within this series of rituals as a lodestar, one that guides us through this arduous, if not, tumultuous journey. Most of us recall that Pandora was given a box with the instruction that she never open it, but she was overcome by curiosity. As a result of her curious nature, out of that box spilled all manner of evils upon the world. What most of us fail to remember is that one emotion remained in the box for her to treasure. That emotion was Hope. We offer our version of the Myth of Pandora's Box as a starting place for each ritual. It may be helpful to reread and review it occasionally.

The rituals in this book are designed to be used in a variety of ways. They can be read by women simply as inspiration, to act as meditative guides when they feel most uncertain. Or, a woman can perform the rituals for herself, setting aside time to come to terms with the difficulties of her journey as only she knows how she truly experiences them. They can also be used by small groups of people, family members and friends who gather together in support of one of their own. Finally, the rituals can be used by larger support groups for women who all share in the common experience of having breast cancer.

This book also contains suggestions for self-care, short daily rites and routines that urge women to pay attention to their wants, needs, whims, and desires in ways that they may never have done before.

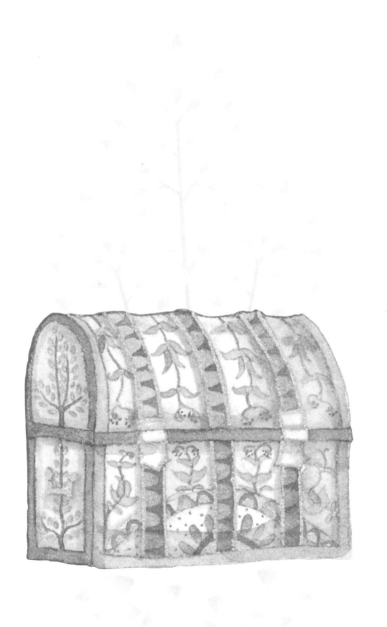

Pandora's Box

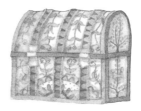

Once upon a time...

there was a woman named Pandora. Pandora's life was going along the way most lives do—with family and friends, work and play. One day, something changed all that.

Pandora found a box.

She wasn't looking for it, mind you. She sort of fell over it. At first, she moved it out of the way and went on about her life.

Then she fell over it again.

"How did that box get in my way this time?" she wondered and pushed it aside.

When she tripped over it a third time, in the same place, she decided she'd better look closely at this mysterious box.

So she sat on the floor with it. It seemed to be a small wooden chest, with brass hinges and latch. When Pandora touched it, she had a strange feeling.

She thought she heard a voice say, "Your life depends upon opening this box, but beware when you do!" Whether the voice was coming from the box or from her, she could not tell. What she was sure of was that she wanted nothing to do with this box.

She pushed it away and got up. She intended to walk away from the box and never think about it again when she heard that same voice, "Your life depends upon opening this box, but beware when you do!" Pandora was frantic. She didn't want to open the box but she loved her life. After a minute, she took a deep breath, bent down and tugged at the heavy brass latch until it opened. She flung back the cover of the box and then...

Oh then, out flew the most dreadful things Pandora had ever seen. Wild things came out of that box. Creatures that ate away at her, that left her weak and shivering and sick. Things that grabbed away from her possessions and abilities she cherished. Then fear came out of that box—fear that sat in her belly and filled her soul. Panic that took possession of her and shook her to her roots.

Pandora cried out in anguish. The box seemed never to empty—more and more things came out of that box—losses, grief, and anger. Each one demanded her attention; each one left her changed.

Then, after what seemed a very long time, the rush of creatures coming from the chest ended. Pandora sat on the floor. She was tired and spent. She was also sad.

"How could such a beautiful box contain such terrible things?" she wondered. If something that looked like a treasure chest could hold such terror, how could she go on?

Wearily, she moved to rise. Then, afraid of being taken by surprise by another terrible creature from the box, she decided to check to see if it were really empty. As she picked it up, sure enough, one more thing emerged.

But this was not a wild creature like the ones that had gone before. No, this was a gentle spirit-like thing—so subtle that at first Pandora was not sure it was real. It brushed past her but did not grab or poke or prod her the way the others had. This one was as soft as a mother's touch on the cheek of her sleeping child. It moved past Pandora's hurt places, soothing them and reassuring her.

...Its name was Hope, and it nested in Pandora and never left.

Rituals for Women Coping with Breast Cancer

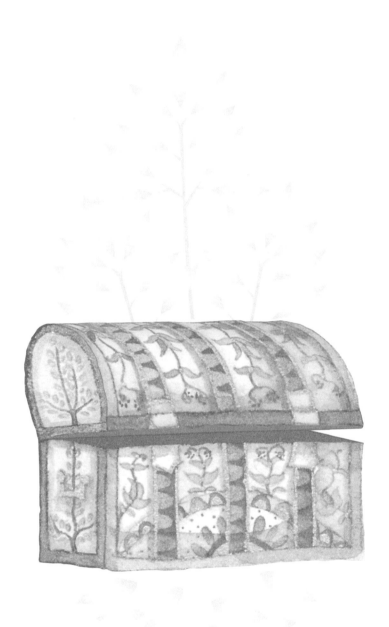

Ritual of Acknowledgment

Acknowledging that One Has Breast Cancer

*"Pandora was frantic.
She didn't want to open the box
but she loved her life."*

The knowledge that one has breast cancer can be so shocking that a woman attempts to protect herself by denying the reality. Even when the information is absorbed on an intellectual level, a person can shield herself emotionally. Many survivors tell us that it was very difficult for them to say the words "I have breast cancer" out loud for the first time. The loss of control, the uncertainty, the fear that these words call forth can be overwhelming. They also say, however, that speaking those words is part of the earliest stage of facing the disease. Doing so opens sources of strength and courage within themselves and allows them to seek comfort and support from others. This ritual provides an opportunity for a woman to utter those difficult words and allow them to become emotionally real to her in the company of people who love her.

1

Materials

A Mirror ❋ Candles ❋ Flowers *(for each participant)*
A Vase *(large enough to hold all the flowers)* ❋ A Talisman

Opening

The woman who has breast cancer welcomes her guests. She asks them for their help and support as she takes a step in the direction of accepting what is happening to her.

An example of a greeting follows:

Friends, I have asked you to come today because I am frightened. It seems as if my body has turned on me. I feel invaded, violated, overtaken by some alien thing that means to do me harm. I often want to pretend it is not true. I am spending so much energy trying to push down my feelings of sadness and fear that I am too exhausted to find the comfort I know is waiting for me—within me.

I ask you tonight to hold me up while I come to terms in a new way with this disease.

I am confident of your love for me, even as I recognize that it cannot protect me from the uncertainty and difficulty I will face in the next few months. What it can do is reassure me that I am not alone and that you each see in me a person with gifts and strength. I hope to draw on your belief in me to rebuild my belief in myself.

At this point we find it helpful for a friend to take over leadership of the celebration.

Litany of Strength

Each person picks up or is given a flower and is asked to think of a strength or special quality he or she sees in the woman who is ill. Then one by one each person names that characteristic and places the flower in the vase. Examples follow:

You have always been able to keep a level head in the face of emergencies. May you be able to use that strength now as you face the crisis.

I have always admired your patience in the presence of anxiety. As you face the uncertainties of your illness, may that patience be among your strengths.

When everyone has named one of the woman's strengths or gifts, the leader presents the vase to her, saying:

This bouquet represents the beauty and strength hidden from you now by your fear and worry. Be reminded of your power. Be reminded of your ability to face whatever comes. You are not alone. You are known by people who love you.

Meditation

The group sits quietly listening to soft music. It might be instrumental music or it might be a song by one of her favorite musicians with words of encouragement. We recommend *In the Arms of the Angels* by Sarah McLachlan.

After the music, the leader asks the group to become centered by becoming aware of their breath. She then asks them to visualize the woman who has called them together. She suggests that they see a ball of light at her center. She asks them to send that image to her. She then asks them to see that light flowing into all parts of her body and again to send that image to the woman who is ill. She asks the woman to be open and receptive to the images that the members of the group are having of her. She asks that the woman try to see herself as they see her.

Saying It Out Loud

The leader hands the woman who has breast cancer a mirror, saying:
We've named your strengths. Now we are here to help you draw on them.

She asks her to stand in the center of the group. The other people gather close to her, resting their hands on her if they are able. The leader asks the group to send the images of the woman with healing light flowing through her. The leader says:

Feel the power of these images of your strength. As surely as your fear is part of you, so is your courage. Look in the mirror for as long as you need. When you are ready, say the words, "I have breast cancer" three times. Remember we are here with you and we believe in you.

Holding Her Up

What happens next depends on the person who has breast cancer. The group, especially the leader, needs to be sensitive to her need. Some women will cry; some will express their fears in a loud voice. Some will be calm, as if released of a burden.

The group should be accepting of whatever expressions of emotion she wants to share with them. They should not attempt to "talk her out of" anything. They need to stand with her (or sit down with her) and let her take the lead.

When she is finished, each person can offer a sign of acceptance and love—hugs work well for expressing those emotions.

The Talisman

The group sits in a circle again. The lights are dimmed and candles lighted. The talisman that the group or the leader has selected is in the center of the table. This talisman should be a small object— a stone, a shell, a pearl, a ring—something portable, something she can wear or carry in her pocket. Something that can be accessible to her to touch when she needs reassurance. Each person touches the talisman to "magic it up," saying: *I am your _____ (friend, lover, sister, daughter, son, brother, etc). Let this be a symbol to you of my love and presence.*

When everyone has touched the talisman, the leader presents it to the woman who has breast cancer, saying:

Receive this sign of our love and presence. Touch it when you feel alone. We will be with you.

Song

We think this kind of ritual ends best when people sing together. It creates a powerful sensual experience that can be recalled when the group is separated.

We have used Marsie Silvestro's *Bless You, My Sister* at times like this—or you might try something lighter like the old standard *Side by Side.*

Claiming Confidence Ritual

Having the confidence that one has made sound choices regarding treatment

"Whether the voice was coming from the box or from her, she could not tell."

When a woman discovers that she has breast cancer, she is faced with making decisions and choices regarding treatments and procedures. This ritual is one that affirms her choices, asks her community to acknowledge her power, and to be with her as she begins treatment. At this point, she has listened to her doctors, consulted experts, and finally made a decision about her course of treatment. Whether it is chemotherapy, radiation, mastectomy, lumpectomy, etc., she needs to believe in her own judgment and have confidence that she has made a choice that is right for her. Shortly before her first treatment, she needs to face her fears regarding medical procedures, her unanswered questions, and any self-doubt she may be harboring. She needs to affirm (and have affirmed) her intuition that she has made the right choice.

2

Materials

A candle ❋ Comforting music
A small bowl filled with large bright beads
A length of string
Also...Each participant is asked to bring an alarm clock
or a noisy kitchen timer (the more raucous the better)

Opening

The woman who has breast cancer or someone who can advocate for her in this difficult time invites a group of people important to her to help her prepare for her first step in treatment. When they have gathered together, she acknowledges that this has been a difficult time but now that decisions have been made, she wishes to proceed with confidence and a sense of positive power over her condition. She also acknowledges her fear and the difficulty in making the choices she has had to make. With this said, she hopes to move forward in an empowered state.

The first phase of the ritual addresses the need to have confidence in one's own internal authority, to have power over one's body and to know what is best for oneself.

The woman who has breast cancer takes up a length of string, selects a bead, and invests it with the power of her intuition. She may say something like this:

I have confidence in my choice. I am an intelligent woman. I have weighed my options. I have sought several opinions. I have asked others to share their experiences with me. I have operated as an agent on my own behalf. I am surrounded by people who care about me.

She slides the bead on the string and passes it to another in the group. Each participant follows her lead, selects a bead and invests it with her notion of the power of self-confidence and intuition. An example follows:

N..., I have confidence in your choice. You are an intelligent woman. You have weighed your options. When I was struggling with..., you helped me. You listened when I needed an ear to hear my pain and my puzzlement. I have long admired the way you ... when ... Know that you are surrounded with my positive presence.

She slides the bead on the string and passes it on.

In this way, all the participants validate the choice the woman who has breast cancer has made by reiterating that she is an intelligent woman, that she has weighed her options, and recounts a brief remembrance of a time when she acted well out of that intelligence and strength.

After everyone has had an opportunity to put a bead on the string, the woman who has breast cancer takes it up. She ceremoniously completes the circle by tying a knot saying,

I let go of my doubts. I have listened and have heard of all the ways those who care about me trust in my choices.

It now becomes a necklace or bracelet, a talisman she can carry with her to remind her of her own wisdom.

Coping With Fear as One Begins Treatment

Most medical procedures are accompanied by fears of the unknown, simple discomfort, intense pain, or isolation. This phase in the ritual prepares the way for coping with those fears. Someone in the group asks the participants to enter into a quiet, reflective state. A candle is lighted to serve as a focal point and soft, comforting music is played in the background.

The woman who has breast cancer sits in the center of a circle surrounded by the participants who sit in reflection with her. The leader asks them to calm themselves, centering their breathing deep in their diaphragms, working to establish a natural breathing pattern. She asks them to focus on the light of the candle and to carry its brightness and heat deep within themselves. After this sense of calm enters the room, she continues:

N . . . , soon you will begin treatment to rid yourself of this terribly disruptive element that has come into your life. Many fears must assail you, keeping you from finding peace. We invite you to name those fears, for in giving them voice, we believe that they become less powerful, even transformed, perhaps, into allies in your own defense.

In response, the woman who has breast cancer attempts to name all of the ways she experiences her fears as she faces her course of treatment. Examples follow:

I am afraid of hospitals: the discomfort of needles, the austerity of white coats, the noises of machines, the glint of surgical steel.

Claiming Confidence Ritual

After each statement, the members of the group respond:

N... , feel our presence in the light of this candle. Let it be a comfort to you as you face your fears. Know that we are with you.

I am afraid of the chemotherapy itself. I understand that it is often accompanied by bouts of nausea and exhaustion. I long for control over the pattern of my days, the responses of my body. I fear having to rely on others who so often rely on me.

(Response)

I fear surgery, anesthesia, and palliative drugs which induce sleep. I fear the loss of control over my own decisions.

(Response)

I fear the aftermath of surgical procedures themselves. I fear that I will not be able to cope with pain, that I will lose control over my sense of self, my sense of humor, my willingness to heal myself when faced with this.

(Response)

I fear disfigurement. Tomorrow I will lose a part of myself and while I know that it is but a part of me, I fear the loss of a sense of wholeness and wellness.

(Response)

Who will take care of my family? Who will feed them and comfort them when I am too ill to carry on in ways that are familiar and loving? I fear the loss of my role as wife or mother or . . . .

(Response)

In this way, the woman who has breast cancer tries to address all the areas in her life that will soon be affected by her treatment.

When it appears that she has finished, the leader reminds her:

N . . . , tomorrow you will physically be alone as you face the ordeal of treatment to cure or cut away at this alien power that has invaded your body. Know that we are with you in spirit. By the light of this candle and the unity of our breathing, we become of one mind despite the fact that distance and geography may separate us.

As a symbol of this unity, each member of the group takes up the alarm clock she has brought with her. In an act of solidarity, they set the alarm to ring at the time when the woman who had breast cancer begins her treatment.

N . . . , this cancer has become a major disruptive force in your life. Each of us goes with you symbolically as you enter into treatment. We set these clocks to ring, to disrupt our lives, so that we might all join with you spiritually, affirming your choices, calling on your internal strengths.

Closing

An act of solidarity is called for as this ritual comes to an end. Encircling the woman who has breast cancer or uniting in a power handshake are just suggestions. All the participants extend their right arms to touch her in some small way, sending positive energy into her as they enact a moment of silence.

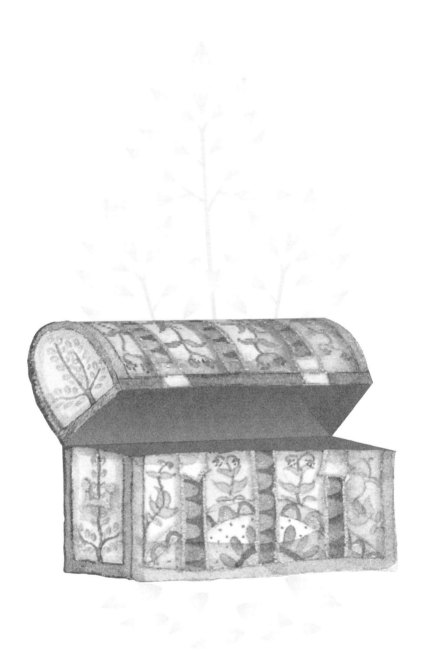

Stream of Emotions Ritual

Coping with the myriad emotions that accompany breast cancer and its treatment

"Wild things came out of that box."

Having breast cancer can unleash a torrent of feelings. Throughout the process of diagnosis, treatment and recovery, emotions surge and tumble like a swiftly moving stream. At times the stream finds a still, protected spot and forms a quiet pool. Other times it runs smoothly, even joyfully. Still other times, it crashes against the rocks, raging in protest over the obstacles in its path. This ritual provides the opportunity for the woman who has breast cancer to express her feelings in a safe and non-judgmental atmosphere.

Materials

Candles that float ✽ Two large bowls filled with water
Fish tank gravel, small stones, or glass marbles
A large pitcher of water ✽ 3" x 5" cards or paper ✽ Pens
Noise makers such as whistles, bells, kazoos, pot covers, etc.

Opening

After all the guests are seated, the woman with breast cancer speaks:

I welcome all of you who love me and have cared for me in many ways. My emotions have become like water, sometimes bursting forth, sometimes eddying quietly, sometimes raging and crashing against the rocks. At times I am optimistic about my treatment and recovery. I also feel fearful, angry, frustrated—and always vulnerable. I ask for your help now in expressing these feelings.

Expressing the Feelings

The woman takes each candle and lights it, expresses her feelings each one and places it in the bowl of water. Examples follow:

This is the light of my anger. I took such good care of myself and I am furious that this has happened to me!

This is the light of my hope. I see so many other women who have survived and are healthy again. I will be too.

This is the light of my loneliness. No one seems to really understand that I feel like a different person and I am isolated from those around me.

This is the light of my vulnerability. If I can have breast cancer, anything can hurt me. I am open and unprotected.

As the woman lights each candle, the group responds:

"Say it, say it, sister!!!" Blow the whistles, cheer, shout, bang the pot covers and generally generate a loud, affirmative response to her feelings.

Accepting the Feelings

Each guest is given a 3 x 5 card or piece of paper on which to write a note to the woman, accepting her feelings. Examples follow:

Dear _____, I accept your feelings of anger. May these feelings ignite in you the fire of determination to become healthy again. All of your feelings are a part of you and flow through you to nourish you. I affirm my love for you and my support.
           Love,

Dear _____, I accept your feelings of hope. May they continue to grow as you continue to recover. I affirm my love for you and my support.
           Love,

Dear _____, I accept your feelings of fear. They are real and important. May you face them with courage and steadfastness. I affirm my love for you and my support.
           Love,

After the group has had the opportunity to write, each guest reads her note to the woman and presents it to her so that she can read them as often as she wants.

Stream of Feelings

Each woman takes the pitcher of water and pours it on the bowl holding the fish tank gravel and stones, saying,

As the water finds its way to where it needs to go, may your feelings find their true expression.

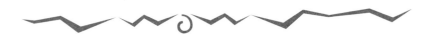

Safe in Our Arms

In order to accept the vulnerability of the woman and to remind her of her safety among those who love her, the next part of the ritual calls for the woman to be cradled in the arms of the group. How this is done depends on the group. If the woman is comfortable and the group is able, she could lie on the floor while the group picks her up to waist level and gently rocks her. Or the group could sit on the floor in a circle with the woman in the middle and place their arms around her and gently sway. Or this could be done standing up. Play soft music such as Sarah McLachlan's *In the Arms of the Angels.*

Naming the Losses Ritual

Naming fears and losses and grieving for them

"Pandora cried out in anguish."

A woman with breast cancer must face a great number of losses in the midst of the turmoil and chaos brought on by her diagnosis. She must do this against the backdrop of a culture that not only denies loss, but expects that she all too quickly "get over" whatever anger, hostility and resentment she may be experiencing because of the cancer. While positive feelings are important, it is a very important for her to name and claim her losses and to grieve over them.

This ritual is designed to empower a woman to recognize her losses as she journeys between discovery to recovery from breast cancer. This is a direct challenge to the way we are taught to think and we do not expect that change will occur immediately or after the experience of just one ritual opportunity. However, we believe that she can become familiar with this process and begin to recognize losses as they come, and see how they can be reshaped as she journeys toward a renewed sense of hope and value.

4

Materials

Candles ✳ *A single flower in a bud vase*
Soft music such as Brahms' Lullaby
A warm garment such as a soft worn t-shirt,
a shawl or scarf, a sweatshirt, or even a receiving blanket

Calling the Group Together

As the group of participants assembles, it may be helpful that a friend of the woman who has breast cancer assumes the leadership role for the ritual. She thanks everyone for coming and invites them to center themselves through a simple breathing exercise which follows:

The participants gather in a circle. They may sit on the floor or on pillows in an atmosphere conducive to quiet reflection and comfort-bearing. The candle is lit and situated in the center of the room where all can see it. Music may be played in the background. Perhaps other lights are dimmed in an effort to tune out the hubbub of the world and its worries.

The leader may say something like this:
May the light of this candle act as a centering force for all of us. Let us focus on the heat of its light and carry that light inward. May it burn within each of us as a reminder of the inner spirit, that center in each of us, where we are truly whole, where we can be at peace.

The leader then asks the participants to join in a series of calming exercises, breathing in and out in an effort to calm and heal.

Naming the Losses Ritual

She may guide them in as simple a fashion as this:

Leader: .... *As I inhale, may I calm my body.*
All respond: ...... *As I inhale, may I calm my body.*

Leader: .... *As I exhale, may I heal my body.*
All respond: ...... *As I exhale, may I heal my body.*

Leader: .... *As I inhale, may I calm my mind.*
All respond: ...... *As I inhale, may I calm my mind.*

Leader: .... *As I exhale, may I heal my mind.*
All respond: ...... *As I exhale, may I heal my mind.*

Leader: .... *As I inhale, may I calm my feelings.*
All respond: ...... *As I inhale, may I calm my feelings.*

Leader: .... *As I exhale, may I heal my feelings.*
All respond: ...... *As I exhale, may I heal my feelings.*

The leader then asks the woman who has breast cancer to read or repeat the following:

As I inhale, may I enter into this gathering, ready to listen to my fears, name my losses, grieve for them, and move toward accepting them as part of the journey toward renewed hope and a healing spirit.

As I exhale, may I enter into this gathering, ready to listen to my fears, name my losses, grieve for them, and move toward accepting them as part of the journey toward renewed hope and a healing spirit.

Naming the Losses

The leader then asks the group to turn its attention to the flower in the bud vase. She may carry it to the place where the candle burns and offer it to the woman who has breast cancer. She images for her friend as many ways as she can that the woman who has breast cancer might envision herself. An example follows:

> *N . . . , imagine yourself as the center of this flower. Each one of its petals represents a different value in your life. This one is Family, this one is your Work World, this one is your Sense of Self.*

The woman who has breast cancer sits quietly thinking of the losses she has experienced most recently in these various areas. For example, she may no longer be able to go to work every day. She grieves for the loss of the companionship of her colleagues, the value she finds in being a member of a team, the socialization in the coffee room. She records her losses on small strips of paper using simple words or phrases so that she might speak of them later.

These are just a few examples of the kinds of things she might think about in terms of her losses:

> *I grieve for my loss of privacy. I have been poked and prodded. I have been cut into, filled with toxins to kill toxins. My body has been invaded by the cancer and invaded by others in an attempt to cure it. I hate this lack of physical boundary, that my physical condition is open to scrutiny by the medical profession, that, at times, I am my disease and I am not N . . . .*

I grieve for my loss of mobility. No longer can I simply come and go freely. I am encumbered by appointments for chemotherapy and radiation, check ups, etc. My life is now ruled by terms dictated by my cancer rather than terms dictated by myself.

I grieve for my loss of get-up and-go. I am so tired. My energy is sapped by drugs and fear. I want to participate fully in the lives of my children. Last night I missed Tracy's soccer game. Tonight I collapsed right after dinner. I no longer have the energy to maintain the fun parts of relationships. I just want to rest.

I miss sex. I grieve for my diminishing sense as a sexual being. I am concerned about my body, that I am no longer attractive and feminine. And while I know that what is beautiful is often culturally imposed on us, I remember feeling good about the way I looked—that I had strong healthy hair and two healthy breasts. I remember the comfort and pleasures of physical intimacy. I want to go back. I want to get it back.

I grieve for the loss of my hair. I feel naked without it, that people know a secret thing about me before I have an opportunity or desire to tell them. I don't want to hide under a turban or scarf, but I also don't want to flaunt my cancer or frighten my loved ones. I want to smell my freshly shampooed hair, I want to frame it around my face, twirl it in my fingers. I want to feel and look like ME again.

The participants in the group are also experiencing losses as a result that their friend has breast cancer. Perhaps she was the one who spearheaded their semi-weekly get-togethers, arranged for the kids' carpool, planned the best impromptu parties or was the quickest to volunteer to lend a hand or an ear in times of trouble. They use this time to record their losses as well.

Sharing The Losses

When the leader senses that the group is ready to move on to the next phase of the ritual, she asks them to listen as the woman who has breast cancer names and shares her losses. Following a format similar to that outlined above, or one that is comfortable for her and the group, she speaks her pain. After each loss is recognized, the group responds.

An example follows:

I miss . . .

All respond: *We hear and respect your grief.*
And we care about your loss.

I hate that I can't . . .

All respond: *We hear and respect your grief.*
And we care about your loss.

I grieve for . . .

All respond: *We hear and respect your grief.*
And we care about your loss.

Following that, her friends are asked to acknowledge their losses as a result of her cancer. For example:

N . . . , I miss the way we used to be able to stay up till the wee hours laughing and sharing family stories. I miss our sense of spontaneity, the way we could behave like kids in spite of our kids.

All respond: *We hear and respect your grief.*
And we care about your loss.

N . . . , I miss your sense of humor. When I could only see the clouds, you buoyed me up when things were darkest. Now I am afraid to burden you with my little troubles in the light of this dangerous disease. I grieve for the way it makes our friendship different.

All respond : *We hear and respect your grief.*
And we care about your loss.

N . . . , I miss our honesty and openness. Now I feel we relate in ways that protect each other from our fears. I am afraid to ask "how" you are doing and I fear that you are afraid to level with me to spare me pain.

All respond : *We hear and respect your grief.*
And we care about your loss.

The Comfort Garment

The closing and the last part of this ritual asks that the participants offer a comfort garment imbued with their love and support. The garment, whether a t-shirt, shawl or baby blanket, is passed from person to person. Each rubs it in a gesture of healing and support. After all have had an opportunity to invest it with a kind of spiritual "magic" or strength, they offer it to her:

N . . . , may you receive this symbol of our love and support. We have listened to your losses. We have tried to bear your pain. Whenever you need to remember that we are here for you, wrap yourself in this garment. Feel its warmth. Feel it as a source of strength and peace. Know that you are loved and cared for.

Celebrating Hope Ritual

Celebrating the Hope of Healing

*"It moved past Pandora's hurt places,
soothing them and reassuring her."*

Fortunately, in the lives of many women who have breast cancer, there comes a time when treatment is finished, when the body has healed, when it is time for the woman to consider herself a healthy woman again. The realization may not come suddenly; it may be a growing sense of energy and enthusiasm, a gradual increase in activity and stamina, an eagerness to make plans for the future. She is not as she was before in many ways—-in many ways she may be better: wiser, stronger, better in tune with her body, better able to take care of herself. At the same time, she faces the fear that the cancer will return. This ritual is designed to celebrate her triumph, to affirm the woman's new and renewed sense of herself as being healthy, and to tame the universal fear of recurrence and put it in a new perspective.

Materials

*The woman collects objects that are meaningful to her that
symbolize what she is now finished with and no longer needs.
For example: a wig or a scarf, a prescription, a card for a
doctor's appointment. We suggest approximately three to five items,
but it could be more if the woman chooses.*

*A large calendar ❋ A plain box or bag ❋ Masking tape
A decorative basket ❋ Friends are asked to bring an item
that has special meaning to them about her, that she can
use to give her support in times of fear ❋ Scarves
Dance music that is lively and upbeat—
Songs such as* I Am Alive, Girls Just Want to Have Fun
Joyful noisemakers like bells, chimes, and drums

Releasing The Past

The woman takes each item that she no longer needs and places it
in the plain box or bag. For each item, she acknowledges the benefits it
provided, but also the pain or resentment she felt. Examples follow:

*This wig enabled me to feel comfortable going out in public. I hated
that it wasn't my own hair. I no longer need it and I release it to the past.*

*This medication helped to kill the cancer cells. It made me feel
so sick I sometimes thought it was worse than the cancer. I no longer
need it and I release it to the past.*

*This doctor's appointment card was the focus of my schedule. I
resented that my life centered on going to the doctor. I no longer*

need it and I release it to the past.

This is a housecoat I bought when I was too sick to feel like getting dressed. I missed my interest in bright colors and clothes that were in style. I no longer need it and I release it to the past.

This is a list of people who drove me places when I was too sick to do it myself. I am so grateful for their willingness, even eagerness, to help me. I resented my loss of mobility, the freedom just to decide that I wanted to go someplace and to go. I still need these friends but not to drive me places. I no longer need this and I release it to the past.

This is an old calendar. I had written on it all the important dates before I was diagnosed with cancer. These are all the things I did not get to do because I was at therapy or at the doctor's or just too tired to do them. I resented the fact that I missed these events. I no longer need it and I release it to the past.

After all the items are in the box or bag, the woman seals it with tape. She may say something like this: *Because of what is in this box, my life will never be the same. I am both resentful and grateful for what these represent. I release them to the past.*

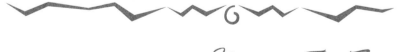

Naming The Fear

Every healthy woman has a fear of breast cancer; every healthy woman who has had breast cancer fears its return. While the fear may never be eradicated, it can be tamed, controlled, befriended, put in perspective. The trick is to stare into the fear without blinking once. In order to assist the woman in her "staring and taming," we ask her to remember the many times in this journey that she was full of fear and in spite of the fear, she kept moving on. The woman names the times she remembers feeling fearful. The group reminds her that she was still able to move on.

Examples follow:

I was fearful when I heard my diagnosis for the first time.

After each statement, the members of the group respond:
You were able to move on.

I was fearful about choosing which treatment to follow and everyone kept saying it was MY decision.

(Response) *You were able to move on.*

I was fearful when I had the surgery.

(Response) *You were able to move on.*

I was fearful about the treatments.

(Response) *You were able to move on.*

I was fearful of the many emotions this brought out in me.

(Response) *You were able to move on.*

I was fearful of all the losses I experienced.

(Response) *You were able to move on.*

I am fearful that the cancer will return. I will be able to move on.

Taming The Fear

Each participant offers a token to the woman with a suggestion as to what to do when she is afraid. These are collected and placed in the basket.

Examples follow:

This is a stone I found while on vacation. Take it and hold it when you feel afraid. May it remind you of your strength and of my support.

This is my favorite photo of you. Take it and hold it when you feel afraid. May it remind you of your exuberant spirit and of my support.

This is my recipe for fudge. Take it and make it when you feel afraid. May it remind you of the sweetness of life and of my support.

This is a bottle of scented bubble bath. Take it and use it when you feel afraid. May the fragrance soothe and comfort you and remind you of my support.

This is your favorite flower. Take it and look at it when you feel afraid. May it remind you of your many facets, of the fact that you are more than your fear, more than your illness. May it remind you of your complexity and wholeness and of my support.

This is some of your favorite tea (or coffee). Take it and drink it when you feel afraid. May it remind you of all the times we have shared over a cup of tea and all the times we will share. May it remind you of my support.

Looking Toward the Future

The woman then writes on the calendar those dates that she is looking forward to like the concert to which she has tickets, and other important dates like birthdays, anniversaries, etc. She explains what each date signifies for her.

For example:

My granddaughter's birthday is October 13. I am really looking forward to watching her open her presents and blow out her candles.

On February 15th, my partner and I are going on a cruise. I am eager to be where it is warm and sunny. I am eager to wear a swim suit and elegant clothes.

On Dec. 24th, we are having family and friends in to celebrate Christmas Eve. I am looking forward to cooking and eating so many of my favorite foods.

Every Wednesday, I am taking my grandchildren to the library for story hour. I am looking forward to spending time with them and helping them pick out books to read.

May 15th is our anniversary. We have plans to go away for the weekend. I am looking forward to our spending time together.

On March 21st, we have tickets to (a play, a concert). This is one of my favorites. I am looking forward to this performance.

Celebrating Hope

This is the time to cut loose, to be exuberant, to rejoice. Put on the music and invite people to dance. Dancing with scarves adds to the sense of festivity. Invite others to ring the bells, blow the whistles, play the chimes, beat the drums. If weather and setting permit, do this outdoors.

Self Care Options

The following suggestions encourage you to pay attention to your wants, needs, whims, and desires, perhaps a strange, even alien concept. These short, daily rites and routines encourage you not only to pay attention but also to see that paying attention is vital to your well-being. You may have to remind yourself that you deserve to indulge your whims and desires. Set aside some time each day when you alone care for you, comfort yourself, pamper yourself.

Ritual of Acknowledgment

❋ Read as much or as little as you want about breast cancer.

❋ Ask a friend to monitor current information over the Web. Let her act as a filter giving you only the information you are ready for at any given moment.

❋ Write down questions you want to ask your doctor.

❋ Take someone with you to medical appointments to act as a second set of ears. Ask that person to take notes.

❋ Seek out a self-help support group.

❋ Do the things that make you feel safer or stronger: wear your favorite clothes and jewelry; take long walks; take baths; hold someone's hand.

❋ Create an image of protection-armor, an aura, a shawl, etc.

❋ Control what you can.

❋ Develop and use affirmations.

❋ Drink soothing teas.

❋ Write your feelings in a journal or talk them into a tape recorder.

❋ Accept help as it is being offered. Seek it out if it isn't readily available.

❋ Practice relaxation exercises.

❋ Listen to your favorite music.

❋ Make friends with your fear; give it a persona that you can talk to, comfort, deal with.

Claiming Confidence Ritual

❋ Develop affirmations of your ability to make good decisions.

❋ Ask questions. Write them down. Take a tape recorder to doctor's visits so you can review the conversation later.

❋ Note other decisions you make that turn out well.

❋ Remember how you adapted when decisions needed to be modified. Affirm your ability to do so again.

❋ Talk with others who have used the same treatment methods you are using. Find out what they did to deal with the side effects and experiment to see what works for you.

❋ Ask your friends and family to make the foods you can tolerate. Keep some in the freezer or on the shelf.

❋ Indulge your cravings.

❋ Make your bedroom a refuge; keep it uncluttered and calm. Retreat there when you need sanctuary.

❋ Create images of other safe places. Go there in meditation.

Stream of Emotions Ritual

❋ Buy some dishes at a garage sale. Smash them to express anger.

❋ Get some sad music that helps you cry it out.

❋ Develop images of yourself moving through fear and panic. (You might be a rocket ship, a subway car, on a horse or a motorcycle. Fear is all around you. You get through it.)

❋ Don't censor yourself.

❋ Draw pictures of what you are feeling or thinking.

❀ Give yourself permission to be angry over the losses and to grieve them. Keep an anger journal.

❀ Spend time outdoors as often as possible. Notice how things that appear to die, are preparing to grow; how a loss in one place means growth in another place.

❀ When the time is right, consider whether or not reconstructive surgery is an option for you.

❀ Rest as much as you need to. Consider this time as germination for new growth.

❀ Create affirmations to say when you are alone. Post them where you will see them often. Acknowledge that for every period of growth in life there is loss.

❀ No matter how much you have lost, you are more than your losses. Create a symbol that represents who you are, that captures the essence of yourself. A painting, a song, a sculpture, a stone, a flower.

❀ Decide ahead of time some ways you will attempt to deal with losses due to treatment—hair is one of the big ones for some people. What makes you feel able to deal with the change? Wigs, shaving your head, turbans, hats, doing nothing?

❀ Make lists that distinguish between losses that are permanent (breast removal) and those that are temporary (appetite, hair, etc.). Visualize yourself restored in those ways.

Celebrating Hope Ritual

❋ Do something special at the end of your treatment according to your own wishes. Go to lunch with a friend. Gather family. Have a special cake or dessert to celebrate.

❋ Gather the people who supported you to thank them for all their efforts.

❋ Have an UN-BIRTHDAY CELEBRATION, one that will celebrate this New Beginning after a year to "reckon with."

❋ Write thank-you notes to health-care providers "who deserve it."

❋ Give yourself the treat of a facial, a body or foot massage to thank yourself for all your efforts and accomplishments.

❋ Plan a gathering where you can give back to those who supported you. You do the preparing and planning as a sign to them of your health and hope for the future.

Additional Suggestions

❋ Visualizations/Meditations - Tapes are available to use whenever you feel "out of control." Make a tape of your own using words and thoughts that are comforting to you. Make a tape of music that you like to help you through sleepless nights or during treatments.

❋ Give yourself permission to receive help from family members and or friends.

❋ Set time aside for yourself. Plan a part of every day just for you.

* Find places that give you the serenity you need. It could be a room in your home, a visit to a church or temple, a walk in the woods, a trip to a lake or pond, whatever helps you connect with all of creation.

* Try to heal old wounds—reconnect with people with whom you have had difficulty in the past. Releasing past wounds can allow you to free yourself up to use the energy for healing.

* Compartmentalize—so often many other issues come up while you are in the midst of the chaos of disease. It is key to learn to prioritize how you will use your energy. Saving most of the energy for your own healing is the most important use of that energy at the time. Compartmentalizing means to put some things "on the shelf" or "the back burner." Remember that Scarlett O'Hara said, "I'll think about that tomorrow."

* Preparing to go to the hospital: Make yourself as comfortable as you can. Take a favorite nightgown, pillow or comforter. Make your surroundings as pleasant as you choose. Take pictures of the people in your life that will comfort you when you see their faces. Do not use the OVERHEAD LIGHT in the room—instead take a little table lamp for "atmosphere."

* Prepare a bag of "special things" that have meaning to you—small gifts from friends, crystals, stones, pieces of material that will make you feel good (like a silk scarf). These are things to make you feel good when you touch or look at them.

About The Prism Collective

The Prism Collective is a group of feminist educators and writers who create resources to make the world a safer and saner place for women.

Because we are committed to social change through educational and spiritual development, we generate materials that we believe make feminist scholarship more accessible to women. We create ways for all women to develop their spiritualities that begin with their own experiences.

We work in a collaborative model which grows out of mutuality and respect for the gifts each of us brings to the community.

We offer the prism as a symbol to remind us that we must look at what is familiar through a different perspective. By refocusing the lens through which we view the world, we see social change as possible.

For years we have created rituals to celebrate women's lives. We hope that as you read and experience these rituals, you will claim your own spiritual power.

Rosalie Muschal-Reinhardt, M. Div.
Barbara S. Mitrano, Ed. D.
Mary Rose McCarthy, M.S. Ed.
Jeanne Brinkman Grinnan, M.S. Ed.

Other Publications by the Prism Collective...

Sisters of the Thirteen Moons
Rituals Celebrating Women's Lives

How can we honor significant moments in women's lives? In the course of a year, the moon goes through its ritual of change thirteen times: New Moon to Crescent to Full Moon. A pattern of change occurs in women's lives as well: Girl to Adult to Old Woman. Throughout time people have noted these changes with ritual celebrations. Our culture, however, has forgotten how to mark these developments and often minimizes their significance. *Sisters of the Thirteen Moons* remedies that lack with thirteen celebrations that imbue women's lives and their everyday experiences with a sense of their sacred meaning. Shared in groups or read as individual meditations, these rituals provide time of tears, laughter and profound understanding.

Journey to a Place among Faith-Filled Women:
A Journal

This journal is designed to help young women journey toward self-discovery, especially toward an understanding of a Spiritual Self. It gives them a chance to travel with a map. Each section poses a series of questions, like signposts, to think and write about. Along the way, young women who undertake this journey will meet both monsters and mentors who will help them learn more about themselves. They will also meet women from both the Old and New Testaments who, like them, had questions and doubts but who, also like them, had courage and faith.

Journey to the Divine Within:
A Journal

An 80-page directed journal for women to discover the life force within themselves. The process for the journey includes Leavetaking, Confronting Fears or Demons, Mentor-Companions, On Sacred Space, The Goddess With Many Faces, The Goddess With Your Face, Celebrating the Goddess and Coming Home.

Choices at the Crossroads

A thirty-minute video produced by Mary Catherine Palumbos when she was in the ninth grade. Seven women students from an urban high school discuss their ideas about themselves and their experiences of racism and sexism in their school and social groups.

Images of the Divine:
A Multicultural, Feminist Perspective

This curriculum is designed for use by teachers of literature, mythology, ancient history, social studies, comparative religions and psychology. Teachers can challenge the patriarchal Western bias of most traditional courses about the myths and rituals of ancient peoples by using the resources and lesson plans. Contains an original Time Line of the Images of the Divine.

A Sociology of Gender Roles Across
Races, Classes and Cultures

This Teacher-Friendly Curriculum includes specific lessons plans for 10 weeks; student resources/handouts ready to copy; teacher resource materials and bibliography. It is designed to (1) look at the process of socialization and its effects on gender roles; (2) introduce the concepts of sexism, racism, and classism as unconscious belief systems, and (3) it discusses ways in which socialization of gender roles has affected both women's and men's lives.

A version of this curriculum with a Christian Scripture base is also available. It is designed to (1) teach or discuss race, class and gender in light of the Gospel message; (2) offer multicultural materials that celebrate the diversity of God's people; (3) offer development of skills to create social justice awareness and actions.

If you would like to order any of these materials, contact:

The Prism Collective
P.O. Box 1042
Webster, New York 14580-7742

716.872.6657 / Fax 716.787.0314
1.800.875.6740

prismcollective@yahoo.com
www.prismcollective.com

"In *Available Hope*, with the ad experience, Richardson remind d loves us—no matter what—and n our own complicated, sometime e hope, and the world is better for

— Sharon E. Watkins, General Minister and President of Christian Church (Disciples of Christ) and author of *Whole: a Call to Unity in our Fragmented World*

"How can we affirm the giftedness of new life in a world that seems to rob us of life in so many ways? This is indeed one of the most urgent demands placed upon those entrusted with the care and development of children. Richardson, a compassionate theologian and a thoughtful pastor, is bold in both her honesty and her hope. She dares give voice to fears even while giving room for hope to resiliently speak for itself."

— José Francisco Morales Torres, Director of Pastoral Formation, Disciples Seminary Foundation

"In these ten essays, the topics of which range from prejudice to divorce, Richardson layers personal narrative, biblical stories, and metaphor to convey both the complexity of our world and the hope that can light our path. Richardson's conversational tone and candor about her own failings make *Available Hope* intimate and thought-provoking, as well as a gentle call to action."

— Kelly Martineau, Seattle-based writer

"Julie Richardson understands that the spiritual life is ultimately forged, not in theological abstractions, but in the daily experiences of life, including talking to a precocious daughter about the joys and challenges of living in the 21st century. Her prose moves the reader along breathlessly, each page crackling with honesty and spiritual insight. She reminds us again that the most sacred thing we can ever do is to tell our story. I loved this book."

— R. Scott Colglazier, Senior Minister, First Congregational Church of Los Angeles

"The most universal truths are almost always the most personal ones. With disarming vulnerability, Julie Richardson invites us into the tenderness of a world at the same time ruthlessly painful and filled with unexplainable grace. *Available Hope* breathes with the authenticity of a life lived with eyes wide open."

— Mark DeVries, Ministry Incubators, Ministry Architects

"Richardson reminds us that although we are so often afraid as we walk through this difficult and terrifying world, still this world belongs to God. Still the world is full of grace and rough beauty. Still the world belongs to our children, who can teach us how to live with hope into the future that lies ahead. Walking with Richardson and her daughter, Maddy, gives me hope in the midst of so much terrible fear in the world today. Through chapters that speak with candor to our most present fears—racial injustice, terrorism, cancer—and to particular events like Hurricane Katrina, September 11, and the Syrian refugee crisis, we find hope is available to us, in one another and in God's love and promises."

— Heidi R. Haverkamp, author of *Advent in Narnia: Reflections for the Season* and the blog *The Vicar of Bolingbrook*

"Julie Richardson is not a fearless narrator, and thank goodness for that. In her willingness to share her imperfections and vulnerabilities, Richardson bears intimate witness to the ways that perfect love casts out fear—even in an age of anxiety."

— Katherine Willis Pershey, author of *Any Day a Beautiful Change* and *Very Married*

"In *Available Hope*, Julie Richardson writes honestly and eloquently about the challenge of parenting in an often terrifying world. Woven through the stories she tells are glimpses of the world she longs for her daughter to inherit: a world not devoid of pain or fear, but a world in which such challenges are met head-on with hospitality, justice, and delight."

— Lee Hull Moses, author of *More than Enough: Living Abundantly in a Culture of Excess*

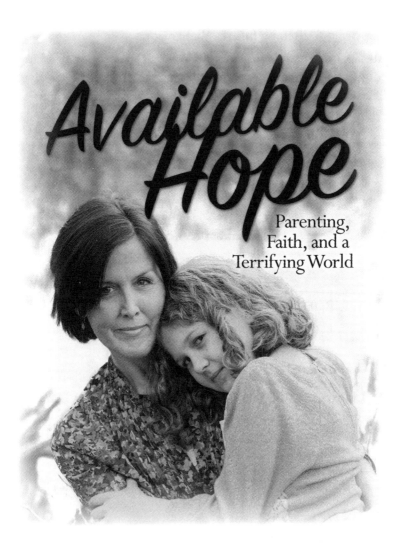

Available
Hope

Parenting,
Faith, and a
Terrifying World

JULIE E. RICHARDSON

CHALICE
PRESS

ST. LOUIS, MISSOURI

Cover art: Jerry McBroom Photography
Cover design: Jesse Turri

ChalicePress.com

Print: 9780827200692
EPUB: 9780827200708   EPDF: 9780827200715

Library of Congress Cataloging-in-Publication Data

Names: Richardson, Julie E., author.
Title: Available hope : parenting, faith, and a terrifying world /
    Julie E. Richardson.
Description: First [edition]. | St. Louis : Chalice Press, 2016.
Identifiers: LCCN 2016018347 (print) | LCCN 2016018904 (ebook)
    ISBN 9780827200692 (pbk.) | ISBN 9780827200708 (epub)
    ISBN 9780827200715 (epdf)
Subjects: LCSH: Parenting—Religious aspects—Christianity.
    Child rearing—Religious aspects—Christianity.
    Parents—Religious life.
Classification: LCC BV4529 .R529 2016 (print) | LCC BV4529 (ebook)
    DDC 248.8/45—dc23
LC record available at https://lccn.loc.gov/2016018347

Printed in the United States of America

CONTENTS

For Madeleine Joy, with all my heart.

ACKNOWLEDGMENTS

I am profoundly grateful for the opportunity to share this book with its readers. The writing of it has been, by turn, exhilarating, exhausting, gut-wrenching, and inspiring. I've never felt more vulnerable in my life.

I owe first thanks to Brad Lyons and the team at Chalice Press. Thank you for believing in what I have to say, and for going above and beyond the call of editors and publishers. You all, truly, have been excellent.

I also want to thank the host of folks who served as volunteer readers along the way. I cannot imagine there having been a half-as-good end result without John and Jeannine Richardson, Joy Lynn Richardson and Zachary Moon, J.T. and Natalie Henderson, Harry Musselwhite, Nancy Chester McCranie, Brian Gerard, Brad Lyons, Clay Mingus, Geoff Brewster, and Kimberly Wrenn.

I am grateful beyond words to all of those who allowed me to tell their stories in these pages. Some of you are named; some of you are not. However, each of you, in your own way, has made me a better person, and I cannot imagine my life without you having been in it.

And, most of all, of course, I thank my beautiful Curly Girl. From the beginning, she knew Mommy was writing a book that would hold in its pages many stories about her. And the truth of it is, without her, there would be no book at all. Always, Maddy, the greatest hope available to me is to be found in you.

AUTHOR'S NOTE

It is one thing to tell your own life story—at least, in part. It is another thing entirely to tell the stories of others.

In the pages of this book, I've written about some painful and difficult things. And, because of that, I've chosen to protect the identities of some of the people of which I've written.

I have often used a person's real name, securing permission if at all possible in those cases. I have, here and there, used pseudonyms. I do not like using pseudonyms as a writer—especially when I am writing about someone that I know well. Using a false name, even with good intentions, seems so disingenuous. Still, sometimes the telling of a story, or the structure of a sentence, just won't otherwise work, and so a pseudonym it is.

I've also chosen, throughout the book in various places, to leave some people unnamed—and I cannot explain that decision other than it felt like the right thing to do to both honor the story and protect the person.

And, finally, I've done my best to use language that is inclusive of all God's children as whole and beloved. If I have failed that in any way, please know that it was not intentional, only my own human inability to ever truly fully encompass the sort of all-embracing and unconditional love the God who created us has for each of us.

INTRODUCTION:
A THIN BLUE LINE

She arrived in my life without warning or expectation, all thoughts of the possibility of her shelved until my heart could again handle conversations about fertility drugs and adoption, exchanged for the far easier and (I thought) lofty goal of becoming the best youth minister I could be.

I learned she existed through a thin blue line on a plastic test stick, instant explanation for recent marked fatigue, dizziness, and nausea. It was just after seven in the morning—and I was home alone, my husband having volunteered to lead a week-long trail camp for teenagers, and therefore out of touch with civilization. I had banked on a lazy mid-summer week with very little to do and not much excitement to be had.

Within minutes of seeing that thin blue line, I'd dialed my younger sister's cell phone, completely disregarding that it was only four in the morning at her apartment in Berkeley, California. I can still hear the quiet pressure of excitement in Joy's sleepy voice, can still sense her smile through the thousands of miles that separated us, as she asked, "Really?!?"

I took five more tests that morning (spending approximately $50 at Walgreen's for my efforts), calling Joy again after the last one to say, "Yep. Really." And then I spent the rest of the day so still, so silent, unable to process what this might mean for my very comfortable, very focused, very fast-paced existence, somehow feeling that the straight plane of my life had tilted into something for which I had no preparation, no map, no instructions—just this vast landscape of unknowing.

Nothing has been the same since that morning—it marked the genesis of a transformation in my life that I am only now, eight years later, beginning to understand. My daughter is the purest expression of God's grace I'll ever know, and in her is all that I have ever longed to be.

We named her Madeleine Joy—the Madeleine after my favorite author, Madeleine L' Engle, and the Joy for my sister. She was born almost a month early via C-section because I'd developed a relatively rare pregnancy-induced liver disease that left me miserable and threatened her safe growth in utero. No words, really, can describe the feeling or concept of your abdomen being sliced open and new life being physically pulled from your very innards. It took mere minutes, and suddenly there she was, held in the practiced arms of my doctor, covered in newborn goo, and absolutely the most beautiful thing I'd ever seen. "Oh, Maddy," I said, my choice of nickname not even a conscious thought, "I love you so much." And then they whisked away her tiny being to make sure all was in working order.

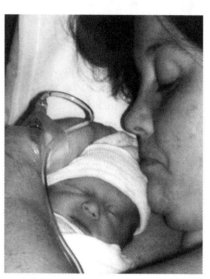

Madeleine and me on the day Madeleine was born

There's a picture of me holding her the day she was born. I'm half asleep, and she's nestled in the curve of my arm between my forearm and my face. I look at that picture and know why I held her that way—I could smell her there. From the very first moment, Maddy's smell was like breathing in mercy. She catches me still, sometimes, burying my nose into the very center of the top of her head, breathing in deep the scent of her.

The next four days are a blur of post-op recovery, futile attempts at sleep, pain meds, and happy visitors. And then, before I felt ready, the hospital sent Maddy and me into the world. Bringing her home was terrifying. The fear felt paralyzing as her dad slipped Maddy's five-pound body into the infant car carrier for her trip home. We left the hospital ten hours later than planned because our girl had been unable to maintain her body temperature. I would have been perfectly happy to stay another night—or several more nights, so afraid and uncertain I was about caring for this impossibly tiny human. My dad, her Papa John, compared lifting her out of the hospital bassinet to scooping a sack of sugar off the shelf at Kroger. It was an accurate comparison.

I've blocked out much of the ride home from the hospital. I know it was winter-dark and winter-cold and that Saturday night traffic clogged the roads of east Louisville. I know I could barely hold myself upright from post-surgery abdominal pain, and I remember not being able to take my hands off Maddy, holding her head up and her body still, fiercely determined she would not fall out of that car seat, unable, at that moment, to recognize that the creators of infant carriers have, of course, designed them to do their job of keeping babies safe while in cars. I bit my lip hard, fought back what felt like shameful tears (*Who cries over taking a baby home?*), and steeled myself against the mad rush of emotions threatening to undo me.

I'd never felt so inadequate, so unprepared, in all my life. And even as I was surrounded by family and friends and skilled caregivers, I've never felt so alone, as if this tiny baby's entire well-being depended solely on me. I've only myself (and perhaps those damn post-pregnancy hormones) to blame for feeling so isolated. My husband rose to the occasion of fatherhood from day one with great skill and even greater love. I had parents who quite literally made life possible those first few weeks, and a sister who, when I called one day in tears, just sure I couldn't be a mother, said, "I'll be there tonight." And she was. Church members cleaned and

cooked and held Maddy so I could shower. Friends walked the dogs and stayed to visit and offered to help in any way they could. I was surrounded by the first inhabitants of what would become, and still is becoming, Maddy's village.

The days held great joy. Still...they were hard, hard days.

And now, sometimes, I wish those hard days back. I could hold her then. I could protect her better when she only weighed five pounds, and when she slept on my chest in the afternoons. I knew she was breathing, and could see for myself, every minute, that she was a perfectly healthy and happy baby.

Now, I drop her off at school, and I watch her walk into that big building, the double doors swallowing her up until they spit her back out again at afternoon carpool, and, every time, my heart pounds harder and faster for a few seconds and a lump rises in my throat, the truth that I cannot, in the end, keep her entirely safe from the world made plain as she skips away from me.

I cannot be the only parent who feels this way.

Maddy has been delivered to a time where, on the one hand, anything is possible and the world is at her fingertips. At age five she could, with one swipe of her tiny hands, "FaceTime" her grandparents, and she first learned to spell her name typing it onto her dad's computer screen. Her school boasts the latest technology and state-of-the-art equipment for everything from music class to the school's black-box theater to the iPad her teacher uses to control the classroom smart board. Her favorite playmates hail from Ethiopia and India, and her typical classroom curriculum includes Spanish lessons. She can text her aunt in Denver, "We're on the way!" while navigating a TSA line at the airport like a seasoned business traveler. She is, in every way, a child of modernity.

But she's also a child of a post–9/11 world. And even if those planes flew into those buildings and those thousands of people died years before she was born, she has inherited the aftermath— lines of

demarcation and hate, after-effects of war, false ideologies of what it means to be patriotic.

The world she lives in is shaped by gun violence, by HIV/AIDS, by the resurgence of heroin, by the curses of instant and mass connectivity, by a widening gap between those who have and those who have not, by systemic racism and excruciating poverty.

Despite her teacher's efforts to be discreet, Maddy can tell you which kids at school go home with a backpack of food for the weekend. She can tell you, too, that it seems like "all the brown kids" are the ones who eat school lunches and "it's mostly kids like me" who bring their own. I had no idea I'd be searching so soon for a way to explain to her that in the town (world, even) she lives in, many more dark-skinned kids live in poverty than white-skinned kids, and those school lunches are necessary for their daily survival.

The world she lives in includes cyber-bullying, internet pornography, human trafficking, and the reality that girls are still assumed to be inferior at math and science, and are, far more often than young boys, defined by their outsides as opposed to their insides. The world she lives in includes genocide, immigration wars, and decided prejudice against the LGBT community.

In other words, the world she lives can be—and often is—a horrifying and awful place.

And, yet....

There is, too, such immense beauty. There are moments of such exquisite and hopeful truth.

"Here is the world," author and theologian Frederick Buechner wrote, "Beautiful and terrible things will happen. Don't be afraid."[1]

But some days I am so afraid for her. Some days it is so easy to focus on the terrible and forget the beautiful.

---

[1]Frederich Buechner, *Beyond Words: Daily Readings in the ABC's of Faith* (New York: HarperSanFrancisco, 2004).

My senior year of college I took a photography class, required for my major in communication. This was well before iPhones or a "Camera Awesome" app, even before digital cameras were readily available to just any person who likes to take pictures. We kicked it old school, and I did so with a manual Canon AE80 with rolls of film that needed to be developed in a darkroom.

I remember only the lesson on "available light," which is exactly what it sounds like—using what light is available—no fancy gels, no up-to-the-minute flash photography, no spotlights or lamps. Available light uses faint sunrise or dying sunset; afternoon rays filtering through an ancient maple; the light of a full moon—*if* the photographer is very experienced and knows just which speed and stop to use. When using available light, you do the best you can with what you've got to capture the moment.

These days, I'm on the lookout for available hope. In the face of all that threatens to undo us, with all the possibility for heartbreak and despair, how do we, as parents, as grandparents, as caregivers, as those who simply care about children, find a way forward that promises them, "You are not alone in this big, scary world. We're with you. And we want for you to know how beautiful this life can be, too."

What hope do we have available to us as we walk alongside our children?

Maddy's buddy Chernet was born in Ethiopia. He was, until some friends of mine adopted him and brought him to his new home to Kentucky, an orphan, lost to some of the worst circumstances you can imagine. There is nothing about Maddy and Chernet that automatically assumes "best friends"—different countries of origin, different native languages, different skin colors, different life experiences, different beginnings. But something in her heart recognizes something in his. And they are fast friends, the joy on their faces as they play a divine prayer for goodness and mercy if there ever was one.

They are available hope—a promise of something beyond all the ways we hurt each other, a promise that all is not lost.

I'm banking on Maddy and Chernet making this world a better place.

Meanwhile, I believe not one of us has a chance of making it on our own, and, in many ways, I've written this book as testament to that. In these pages, I want to bear faithful witness to the relationships and experiences that lead me to hope, that beckon me to trust the inherent goodness of the world, despite any evidence to the contrary. I want to share the hope available in my own life, broken though it may be, so that perhaps the hope in yours might be more evident, more discoverable, and eventually fully known.

I am no parenting expert, I assure you (and I don't trust anyone who claims to be). My efforts to be Maddy's mom to the best of my ability are fraught with mistakes. The eight years since she's been born have held for me a significant career shift, loss, illness, divorce, and, as with all of us, the whole host of other challenges that go along with being alive.

Some of those stories I share in these pages. People and experiences and events that pre-date Maddy's existence, but that have an effect on her life because they've impacted her mother, just as I've been impacted by the lives of my mother and father, and they theirs. Not a one of us rises to the occasion of caring for a child without all that has shaped us—that which has been

Maddy and Chernet

good and that which has not been—coming to bear on how we love and guide our children.

And so I simply tell you, this is my story, so far, of what it has meant to be a mother, a parent, a caregiver to a child, in this world we live in, and how my life, as I understand it perched at age 40, has led me to mother my daughter with hope, even when it seems impossible.

Chapter 1

INNOCENCE

I could have been born in the back of a tow truck—or, perhaps, in the back of a Thunderbird. In the end, though, it was in a hospital.

It was Memorial Day 1975, in McGehee, Arkansas. My parents lived in McGehee at the time, and had been on a holiday picnic with my dad's sister Joyce and his mom (Nana, always, to me) and my parents' Schnauzer Cassie (named for Mama Cass). Mom was very pregnant with me, her first child—so much so that she was scheduled to be induced the next day at a hospital in Stuttgart, about an hour east of Little Rock, where Nana and Aunt Joyce lived. So, after the picnic, as evening approached, they all decided to head to Little Rock for the night, and then my folks would be closer to the hospital the next morning.

A half-hour into that drive to Little Rock, my parents' 1973 Chevy Impala died. Nana and Aunt Joyce assumed they'd stopped for a drink or gas and kept going. No smartphones for them to call one another. No Siri to check for any nearby help. And it was getting dark, so it was very fortunate Mom and Dad found a farmhouse with the lights on and people inside willing to call a tow truck. The nearest town was Pine Bluff, and the tow truck driver agreed to take them there along with towing the car. As they climbed into the tow truck, my parents' banker pulled up next to the scene, he and his

wife having, serendipitously, been on a holiday outing themselves, and they volunteered to take my parents back to McGehee.

As Mom exited the tow truck to get into the banker's car, her water broke. This, as you might imagine, raised the stakes and everyone and everything sped up a bit. I'd love to know how fast that banker drove—and what his wife thought of a woman in the early stages of labor in the backseat of the family car.

Once back in McGehee, another set of friends took them to the hospital in Stuttgart. One of the friends had been a medic in Vietnam, and he pulled up to their house in a Thunderbird, towels and sheets stacked between the bucket seats—ready to deliver me, I suppose, if necessary. This was not all that reassuring to my mother, I'm told.

Mom finally checked into the Stuttgart hospital around midnight, at which point I decided that, for all everyone's haste in getting Mom to a labor and delivery unit, now I could take my own sweet time in arriving. I gave Mom and Dad both a hard way to go during the wait, and, so the story goes, Mom was so pale from loss of blood by the time my difficult delivery was over that Dad took one look at her and passed out in the hospital hallway. Nana saw him hit the floor from the waiting room and screamed, "Is Jeannine dead?!?"

Mom was not dead, but Dad did have to join her in the hospital recovery room until he recovered from his unexpected swoon. The next day, Mom says, before folks asked, "How are you?" they asked, "How's your husband?"

My birth story is one of the most remarkable stories of my existence—and I had no idea it was happening. Strangers, friends, family, circumstances—all of this worked together to bring me into this world. So much could have gone horribly wrong. But it didn't. There's no identifiable reason for this, other than maybe, that day, the inherent goodness of the universe won over and against tragedy or heartbreak. If this is the case, I am simply quite

lucky—because goodness doesn't always seem to win. And tragedy strikes at random all the time.

All I know is that it happened. And it was all okay. And from day one I have been loved without measure. No matter broken-down cars or screaming grandmothers or fainting fathers. No matter what, really.

And this has made all the difference in my life.

❧ ❧

Place and family have been everything to me, the geography of my existence beginning in the rivers and creeks and woods of rural Arkansas, where the Richardsons have been for several generations.

When I was very young, I could have ventured inside any convenience store or diner in the tiny Ozark town of Amity, identified myself simply as one of R.J.'s grandkids, and receive a warm welcome—even though I never knew R.J. Richardson[1] in person, only through the stories I've heard my whole life long about my paternal grandfather who died long before I was born. Sometimes, I imagine if there is truly an afterlife in which we recognize the cloud of witnesses that has gone before us, the first thing I'll do is look for him. And when I find him, I'll say, "I missed you."

In whatever house we lived in as I was growing up, there was always a wall reserved for framed cross-stitched tapestries Mom made of every state we'd lived in thus far. Arkansas. Kansas. Then Texas. Tennessee, because that's where Mom is from. And then, most importantly for me, Georgia. Though I now call Kentucky home, a small town in north Georgia is where I learned what it meant for the soul of a place to get in you, to form in ways both positive and negative who you are and who you will become.

---

[1] "R.J." did not stand for anything. It was just "R.J."—I'm told that the sergeant who once checked R.J. into basic training at Pine Camp in Pine Mountain, New York, did not find this to be acceptable, demanding repeatedly that R.J. tell him what the initials stood for—to, of course, no avail.

Winder, Georgia, population some 10,000 when I moved there in the winter of 1989, is situated just off State Highway 29, some 50 miles northeast of Atlanta. Winder's greatest claim to fame might be that it is the hometown of Senator Richard B. Russell Jr. (1897–1971), namesake of a Senate office building and a leader in the Southern opposition to the civil rights movement.

First called Snodon by the Creek Indians who called it home hundreds of years ago, then Jug Tavern by white settlers who arrived in the late 1700s, Winder finally became Winder in 1893, about the time that the Gainesville Midland Railroad and the Georgia, Carolina, and North Railroad both built tracks through the city. Jug Tavern became a stop on the Atlanta–Athens line, population and commerce boomed, and the city of Winder was born.[2]

Almost one hundred years later my family would arrive, as Dad had been called to be pastor of First Christian Church (Disciples of Christ). That was some twenty-five years ago, and though a great deal in Winder has changed since then, you can still find families who have known each other for generations, businesses that date back, even if loosely, to its Jug Tavern days, and two sets of railroad tracks that still define the city's business and social center. You'll find thick red clay (instead of black soil) beneath you, sky-high pine trees above you, and little lakes and green space around you—enough that a kid can still explore the woods without venturing too far from home.

It was, when I knew it best, a racially segregated town. By and large, white folks lived on one side of the train tracks, and black folks lived on the other. Pockets of extreme poverty existed, too, especially "out in the county"—Barrow County. It was a while before I really understood this. I'd come from a large public middle school in south Texas where the Hispanic kids—mostly Mexican—stood equal in number to the white kids, with just a smattering of black kids among us. Maybe I was just younger, and therefore oblivious, but

---

[2]My own eighth grade history class being fuzzy in my memory, I am grateful to the city of Winder's website, where I was able to double-check the history I thought I remembered.

the hallways of my big Texas middle school seemed less confining, less divided, less built on ancient and unspoken social rules.

My sister Joy and I both attended what was at the time the only public high school in Barrow County. And Winder-Barrow High School was, in many ways, a reflection of the town itself: social structures and roles defined by what sport you played and how well, what church you went to, who your folks were, what part of town you lived in, and what color your skin happened to be. I speak in generalities here, and there were certainly exceptions, but by and large, this is how I remember things.

And across the street from Winder-Barrow High School, sat First Christian Church.

It is no overstatement to say that First Christian Church was—and is—a significant defining force in my life. I know every of inch of its space, every nook and cranny, every spot where a preacher's kid could disappear with a good book for a while as her dad finished up a meeting.

First Christian smells like the oil used to keep its wooden pews shiny, and like the parade of Easter lilies that grace its wide chancel every spring. First Christian tastes like Miss Sandra's homemade lemon squares that showed up at every potluck, and like the hundreds of chickens boiled and pulled apart every fall for the Christian Men's Fellowship chicken stew sale. First Christian sounds like the mighty Moller pipe organ the sanctuary holds, full stop in the midst of "Joyful, Joyful, We Adore Thee," or a quiet piano solo of "Silent Night" on a dark Christmas Eve, with only candles lighting the way to the joy of Christmas Day.

The women and men of First Christian ordained me into ministry. I was married there. I sang more Sundays than I can count from its choir loft, and, more important than all these things, perhaps, I learned there what it means to be part of something bigger than myself. It wasn't perfect, not by any means, and there were certainly

people and situations that made life difficult for a preacher and his family. But it was home.

Life seemed so very ordinary then.

It's only in retrospect I am able to see the way things came together, or sometimes didn't. The way that small town and that church and those people made me who I am. The way, too, my parents protected Joy and me from the hard things in life as best they could, and how, when they couldn't protect us, they showed us how to navigate the difficulty or pain with grace and persistence. This mattered so much when I began to learn how terrifying this world can be. How brutally it can wear on a person. How random evil is. How safety is never a guarantee.

∾ ∾

I was a sophomore in high school the January night that Tom Brokaw announced Operation Desert Storm, the combat phase of the Gulf War, had begun. Prior to Desert Storm, I had been ignorant of any conflict or complicated relationship between the United States and the Middle East. And the whole idea of a nation at war was simply a historical one to me—way back in the dark ages of the 1970s, most recently.

I've no idea how other fifteen-year-old girls around the nation reacted to Desert Storm, and perhaps my own reaction would have been different had I been born to other, less globally aware parents, but it was, for me, a pivotal moment in my adolescent consciousness. I distinctly remember saying to my dad, "This is the United States, and we don't go to war anymore!"

But we did.

Operation Desert Storm is also the first time I remember intentionally turning to writing as a way to work out what I was feeling. I wrote a series of fictional journal entries, all of them imagining a brother named Gerald being deployed to Iraq, and then being reported as one of the some 145 U.S. troops killed in action.

Later that spring my fictional journal entries won an award from the city of Winder. I was proud then, excited about the monetary award that came with the recognition. Now, I think how sad it was—that such global terror led to a $100 check and my name in the city paper, along with the text of the fictitious journal series.

But hasn't this always been the case? Before and since? Great novels, epic poetry, heartbreakingly beautiful music—so much of it is created in response to things that have gone horribly, painfully, tragically wrong.

Meanwhile, during that war, my dad gathered every week with various folks around town to pray for peace. It was all, I now believe, my first lesson in not giving in to the way things are, in hoping, trusting, that something more whole and beautiful is possible. In the face of chaos and death, I wrote. Dad prayed. Neither of us could stop the fighting, or unwind centuries of unrest in the Middle East. But we could let the world know we weren't okay with it all.

⊱ ⊰

I file the things I worry about as a parent into two categories. You might call them macro vs. micro concerns. Or global vs. local concerns. I call them "The World" vs. "My World."

In "The World," I worry about things like the 2013 Boston Marathon Bombing—a wonderful, celebratory, annual, amazing, family and fun-oriented event turned complete nightmare. Or the 1995 bombing of the Murrah Federal Building in Oklahoma City. Things like this sometimes make me nervous in large crowds. At huge public events. Truthfully, things like this terrify me if I dwell too long on their possibility, because I cannot control extremist bombers.

There is absolutely nothing I can do to protect Maddy from such an event.

I also file in this category things such as a plane crash at the Lexington, Kentucky, airport in 2006. Comair Flight 5191 was

scheduled to fly from Lexington to Atlanta one August morning. It crashed during takeoff at Bluegrass Airport, and all but one of the fifty passengers died. At the time I was serving a church in Lexington, and it didn't take long for the connections between church members I knew and loved and people on that plane to become clear. The entire town settled into deep grief.

There is absolutely nothing I can do to protect Maddy from such an event.

War. Flood. Famine. These great forces and significant game changers of history—and of the story of my Christian faith—they cannot be controlled. They can only be lived through.

In "My World," I file car wrecks. Senseless accidents. Terminal illness. In My World, I file the sorts of everyday tragedies that can destroy a life, wreck a person, change the entire trajectory of a family's existence.

In April 1994, my first year at Berry College in Rome, Georgia, came to an end. As is typical of college campuses, I had to move out of my dorm for the summer, and the Saturday morning after my last classes, Dad came to pick up me and my stuff. I was heading home for a few weeks before my summer work at a church camp began.

By the time we'd finished loading up the car, it was lunchtime, and so we stopped at the local Applebee's for a quick bite. I had the Oriental Chicken Salad. I do not remember what Dad ordered. I suspect he doesn't either. And I remember the Oriental Chicken Salad, a dish I loved then, quickly turning to sawdust in my mouth as Dad spoke, quietly, the words coming slowly as he tried to speak calmly, "Julie, there's something important you need to know before we get home. Your mom has been diagnosed with breast cancer. She is going to have surgery soon. A mastectomy. And then she is going to have chemotherapy and radiation."

My entire world shifted, spun, shook at Dad's words. I now knew very real and very deep fear. And I remember being very quiet.

Very still. A typical reaction for me in the midst of very painful or difficult or unsettling news. Would my mother die? This was my primary question, and one my mother faced head on as soon as I got home a couple of hours later. "Julie," she said, sitting on the edge of the queen bed she and Dad shared, covering my hand with hers, and speaking with such caring forthrightness "This does not mean I'm going to die."

That may have been one of her finest moments as a mother. And though I wouldn't know it until years later, it taught me a great deal about how we face the things we hope to never face in life. We do it honestly. With conviction. With grace and strength. And with a willingness to tackle the hardest and biggest questions first.

In the end, my mother kicked cancer's ass. Still, *still,* in My World, I file breast cancer. I do my best to eat relatively healthy; I exercise; I get regular breast checks and annual mammograms. But I fear it. Especially as I approach the age my mother was at diagnosis.

In My World, too, I file the things that can happen as the result of one bad choice—things such as drug addiction or alcohol poisoning or an STD from careless or unprotected sex. Things I've watched teenagers battle, things I never want my Maddy to have to face.

And, in My World, my greatest fear is losing my daughter.

✌ ✍

One summer, I took a group of middle-school youth on a mission trip to the Heifer Ranch in Perryville, Arkansas. Heifer Ranch is an outreach and service learning center of Heifer Project International,[3] founded by an American farmer named Dan West. The Heifer Ranch is a fully functioning livestock and produce farm, and it hosts groups from all over the world who want to come to learn about how sustainable living can combat hunger and poverty.

---

[3]Heifer Project International is headquartered in Little Rock, Arkansas. I urge you to learn more about their work at www.Heifer.org

For groups of young people who visit, one of the options is to participate in a "high ropes" course experience together. I'd signed up our group of a dozen kids, and the morning the course was on our agenda, everyone woke up raring to go, ready to face the challenge.

The kids all went first, us adults hanging back while they went at it with the clear-eyes-and-full-hearts bravery typical of most middle schoolers. And we smiled as they worked through the ropes and bridges and platforms strung high up above us, helmets and cables and steel D-rings their safety gear as we helped belay them up and down the course.

When my turn came I was chomping at the bit to go—and I hopped on the first rung of a forty-foot telephone pole ready to scurry right up to the course's first element. Only, halfway up—completely unexpectedly—I froze. Solid. Couldn't move. And no amount of cheering or pleading from my youth group below could convince me I could do it. Eventually, I gave up, quietly asking the course instructor to help me down. It was a moment I'd rather forget.

But I didn't forget. And I didn't give up. Several years later—and, I might add, several failed attempts at redeeming myself on other ropes courses later—I decided I'd had enough, and so with every ounce of courage I could summon, I grabbed two trusted friends and headed out to a nearby camp that had recently redone their high ropes course—higher than any course I'd ever attempted, and I knew it.

Our course instructor knew I was scared, but he also knew I was doing this for myself, and he wasn't about to let me chicken out. He got us through the safety talk, the preparation, and instructions quickly and efficiently, and after letting one of my friends go up first, he insisted I go next. On automatic pilot, fighting every impulse to just walk away, I put my foot on the first steel staple in the very, very, *very* tall pole up to the course, and pulled myself up. And, as I had done every other time, about twenty feet up I froze. No amount of gentle encouragement from either friend or from the instructor could get me to budge. And, then, my friend

still on the ground said, "Julie, what if I just tell you what to do? What if you just close your eyes and I just tell you what to do?"

Close my eyes, I thought? *Are you kidding me? No way!*

And then something inside me gave way—fear of falling, fear of failing, fear of losing control— it all gave way to this feeling that I could do this, that I could trust these people to keep me safe, that it would be okay. And so I closed my eyes tightly, took a deep breath, and nodded.

"OK, good," my friend's voice, now guiding me, said. "Now, move your right foot up one staple; OK, good, now move your left hand up one staple; OK, now move your right hand," and so on and so on, and all the way up, my eyes remained shut and I blocked out everything except the sound of my friend's voice guiding me up the pole.

I did it.

There are days, moments, in this journey of being me, of being Maddy's mom, that I freeze. Think I cannot possibly do it. There's too much that could go wrong. Too much that I cannot control. Too much that I am not sure of.

My college roommate, Kimberly, has two boys just a bit younger than Maddy. And she once told me the only way she knows to describe the intensity of loving your child is this, "It's like you reach in and take your heart out of your body, and then just let it just walk around, unprotected and completely vulnerable."

There are days when I want to snatch up my heart in the form of her and wrap it all back up safe inside me.

But this is such foolishness.

Because, you see, control—in the form of safety or otherwise—is such an illusion. And certainty is so very illusive. Evil happens. Chaos ensues. Awful pain strikes us close. And, given these truths,

we have two choices—to live in fear, or to live in love. To live frozen and afraid, or to live trusting that the universe, as it has been created, has been created for good, and all along the way there are voices, should we choose to hear them, whispering, "OK, now, one foot forward. You can do this!"

I have two plum lines that I measure against when writing or speaking: (1) Could you say that with any authenticity if you knew the mother of a child killed at Sandy Hook Elementary School was going to read/hear it? And (2) Could you say it to the face of a survivor of the Holocaust?

Because, in truth, my life has been a privileged life. And in any moment of heartache, I have never been entirely alone. I have known, even in despair, immense beauty in all sorts of ways and through all sorts of people. And because of all this, I can say, "I believe in the inherent goodness of the universe." And I do, even on the days when I want very much for the universe to go to hell because, dear Lord, it can just be so awful.

On the morning of the fourteenth anniversary of 9/11, I posted a picture to Facebook of my cousin Alison and me. It is a photo taken by one of our parents at a waterside park in New Jersey. And behind us rise tall and strong the Twin Towers, some dozen years before those towers would fall from the scheme of terrorists.

I had, until that morning, never spoken with Maddy about 9/11—mostly because I wanted to shield her from its horror, protect her innocence of such things as much as I could. But also because...*how?*

She saw the picture as I posted it, and she asked, "What's that, Mommy?" And I told her that it was me and my cousin, and the picture was important because it was taken while those towers were still there, and they were gone now.

Maddy was quiet for a moment, and then she said, "Mommy? Are those the buildings those planes flew into and all those people died?"

I was stunned. I looked at her for a moment, took a deep breath, and said, "Maddy, yes. But honey, how do you know about that?"

"Oh, I've heard people talk about it at school," she said. "It's sad how those planes accidentally flew into those buildings."

"*Accidentally.*"

I couldn't let it go, "Oh, Maddy, honey," I said, "it wasn't an accident." And I told her—about how some people who were really angry and evil and sick did it on purpose. Her response did not surprise me, and I will certainly never forget it, "Mommy! How could there be that much evil in the world?!?"

In her sweet innocence, having been loved and held safe her whole life, she could not fathom it. Could not understand how such a thing could have even happened unless it was an accident. And just like that, her innocence about this particular thing, a horrific moment when everything changed, was gone.

Eventually—even if we have been lucky enough to have been born into lives in which our innocence remained intact for while—we all lose our innocence. It is not possible entirely to shield ourselves or anyone around us from the ugliness of the world.

And so maybe the most we can do is face it together, shoulder to shoulder, with that courage and grace and conviction Mom taught me about as she faced cancer. So our children learn they are not alone. So they learn we will walk with them into whatever's coming.

I have been taught, through these people and experiences and stories I've shared, that (1) God loves me...no matter what, and (2) God will never leave me...no matter what. I say these same things to Maddy as often as I can, and I try to show them to her even more.

Because, above all, knowing what will become of whatever scraps of innocence she still carries, I want her to know that she will not face anything this world hands her alone...or unloved.

Chapter 2

BABIES

Crawford Long Hospital,[1] in the heart of Atlanta's busy downtown, is not the city's major trauma hospital, but it is a typical downtown, major metropolitan hospital in that anyone, from any walk of life, could happen through its doors. You'd be just as likely to see the mayor of Atlanta arriving for cancer treatment— and I once did—as you would a homeless person seeking help with a wound or virus. CLH is named for Dr. Crawford Williamson Long, a Georgia physician known as the first physician to use ether anesthetic.

I spent 3 months at CLH as a chaplaincy intern, midway through my seminary journey. I was all of twenty-four years old and felt woefully inadequate for the tasks I was charged to do: standing at folks' bedsides while a physician said, "There's nothing more we can do," or holding the hands of worried family members in the ER, asking, "Who can I call for you?" when things became too much for someone to handle alone.

During my time there, I was assigned first to "the kidney floor"— the hospital's renal unit, which mostly consisted of patients who were noncompliant diabetics. My second assignment was Labor and Delivery. A happy thing, right? Not always. Especially not at CLH—the premier referral hospital in the city for high-risk

---

[1]CLH is now known as Emory University Hospital Midtown.

pregnancies. I saw some of the worst heartache you can imagine during the days and nights I spent on the Labor and Delivery floor.

I will never forget one particular Tuesday.

The head nurse working Labor and Delivery was, at the outset, all business. She had short blond hair, dark-framed professional eyeglasses, and perfectly pressed scrubs. She always had a clipboard. She spoke in terse sentences and had a no-nonsense approach to her daily rounds. I learned to like her in my time at CLH, perhaps because it didn't take me long to discover that her gruff exterior held a heart that cared deeply for her patients. Still, I was generally happy to leave L & D visits to my two female colleagues in the chaplaincy office—both much older chronologically and in life experience than I at the time.

One day, though, I could not avoid her. I was "on call," and that meant if someone paged, I answered. No questions asked.

She paged.

As I stepped off the elevator onto the polished wooden floors of the maternity ward, her usually brisk façade was instead pained and compassionate. Quickly she pulled me into a quiet corner to tell me about the young woman a few doors down the hall who'd just delivered a dead infant. I cannot recall her words exactly. I blocked them out long ago. As I tried to process "three months premature," "stillborn," and "positive for marijuana," she led me to the patient's room.

Inside the plush comfort of a high-end maternity suite, I found a teenager, propped up on a stack of pillows, knees drawn up against her chest to hold the body of her newborn son. The smile she offered when I entered appeared surreal, unnatural, and inappropriate given the situation, and as she held him up for me to see, the nurse said, "She'd like for her son to be dedicated, and I need you to talk with her about what she wants, and then do whatever that is. I need you to perform a service of dedication." I nodded, not taking my

eyes off the tiny body I was looking at, wrapped in a standard-issue hospital receiving blanket, no cap covering the little head.

"Isn't he beautiful?" the mother asked, and I nodded again, forcing back the bile rising in my throat, my legs cement and my heart pounding. On the couch, across the room from where I stood, sat a toddler. "Come see your little brother!" she demanded, in a high, strange voice. He came—unwillingly, his feet dragging and his movements slow, his eyes downcast—only to be forced to hold the body I could barely look at.

And I fabricated an excuse to leave the room—both because I could not take the scene much longer, and also so I could race down to the chaplain's office, five floors and a long stretch of hallway away, to find an appropriate liturgy for such a thing.

I remember holding that tiny boy, so small I could cradle him easily with my own two hands held together—his features soft and hardly formed, miniature hands and feet, button nose and barely there black lashes. For what seemed like hours I held him, automatically responding to his mother's questions, listening with one ear toward the door where hushed hallway conversation between nurses and hospital security indicated dead boy's mother would likely face charges for her drug use before the day was over. Somehow, I found the words to dedicate the child to God and the presence of mind to sign a dedication certificate for posterity.

Later that evening, sitting at a nursing home dinner table with my fiancé's family as we celebrated an early Thanksgiving dinner with his Alzheimer's–ridden grandmother, I found myself unable to respond to everyday conversation, unable to taste whatever food I was absently stabbing with my fork, unable to see the point to anything around me, unable to escape the feel of that tiny lifeless body in my hands and the sight of him in front of my face. When a child is born that soon, too soon, it's obvious the child hasn't been fully formed, and in his sweet round face I'd been able to see the signs of skin beginning to tear apart, to decay with absence of

life. He haunted me for weeks, that little boy. And some days does still. I think of him with no identifiable trigger—just a persistent memory that rises at random in my consciousness now and then.

If Operation Desert Storm shattered any notion I had the world was a safe place, holding that lifeless little boy swept aside that rubble and left a gaping hole in my heart, a spot where, still, I unwillingly harbor the things in this world that horrify.

≈ ≈

Some fifteen years later, I held another baby in my arms, this one full-term and born into strong, loving, and welcoming arms. And as I held my precious niece, Ruby Lynn, for the first time, just a few days old, and I whispered, "Hi sweet girl, I'm your Tatie," into her soft and perfect ears, it was obvious how full of life and health and promise she was.

I'd flown that day from my home in Louisville to her home in Denver. Ruby had been born six days earlier, and I was eager to meet her and check on her mom, my younger sister.

It was Friday, December 14, 2012, and as I'd waited to board my flight, I'd stood, silent, with hundreds of other folks in the airport's Southwest Airlines terminal, staring at the television monitors above us. One played CNN, another MSNBC, another Fox News, another a local network affiliate—all of them reporting the same thing: that that morning, in Newtown, Connecticut, twenty students and six of their teachers and leaders at Sandy Hook Elementary School had been murdered.

I got on the plane shaking, desperate to call home one more time and check on my own sweet girl, five years old at the time. Hearing her tiny voice through my phone calmed me enough to take the flight. At the other end of the trip stood my dad, ready to take me to my sister's place, and I almost fell into to his arms in my heartache.

His own grief was palpable, and all over Denver International Airport was this eerie sense that something, somewhere, was very, very wrong.

And it was.

I wrote these words on the plane that evening, crammed up against my chosen window seat, my fingers unable to put to paper fast enough the sorrow boiling over in my heart:

> *For the children who have been lost, my soul twists with grief. For the children who have survived and will never be quite as innocent as they were this morning, my heart aches. For the mothers and fathers who sent their sons and daughters to school never to see them alive again, I am sickened and numb with even the possibility of such pain. For those who loved the adults who I imagine screamed, "No!" and fell dead anyway, I am so sad. For the first responders and emergency crews and policemen and rescue workers and medical personnel, I offer thanksgiving and pray that they will find a sense of peace on the other side of the hell they have seen this day…*

> *…[I]f there is anything the love of God has taught me, it is that we are connected by God's breath and spirit and presence in each of us. And just as God's heart is breaking today, so ought all ours break—whether this nightmare hits close to home or not. This is not isolated tragedy and violence. This happens every day, somewhere. And, until we rise up as human beings and say, "No more!" it will continue to happen. This I believe, too.*

> *There will be, in the days ahead, more chatter about this than any of us is able to process. And there isn't anything that can fix it. And how in the world we are to proclaim the joy of Jesus' birth, the grace of God's love in the face of it, I'm not quite sure.*

> *And so I fall back to promises that have made me who I am— that death does not have the last word; that God is here, in the*

*thick of blood and screams and shattered lives; that we can do
better, because we have been made for love; that somewhere,
somehow, out of this it is possible to live into goodness and
mercy; that we are not alone; and that, always, there is hope.
Those promises may not mean much in the darkness. But I
cling to them this night.*

And I confessed to Ruby Lynn, as I lifted her into my arms, "How
I need you this day, baby girl. How the world needs the hope your
new life brings."

The next day, writing while she napped, my own soul better able
to hold both the pain of Sandy Hook and the joy of Ruby, I wrote:

*I sit perched on a stool, writing at a high-top table, and Ruby
is at my right, my foot rocking her bassinet. She's murmuring
and cooing in her sleep, her tiny hands waving in the air from
time to time and her eyes fluttering open and then quickly
closing again every once in a while as if she's just checking to
be sure I'm still here. It seems so obvious to note her life is just
beginning. But sometimes the obvious needs recognizing. So
much beautiful potential rested in her eight-pound self, even as
so much beautiful potential has been destroyed at Sandy Hook.*

*I have a friend who is a Sunday School teacher—worried that,
tomorrow, the third Sunday in Advent, he will not have the
right words for the children in his class when they ask him,
"Why?" about Sandy Hook. I am not sure there are "right"
words. I do know that there are words that begin the slow
and agonizing process of healing. These are words that assure
us the angels have not left us and that God is still God. These
are the words I want to whisper into Ruby's dreams tonight.*

ॐ ॐ

Perhaps for the rest of my life I will be unable to separate Ruby
Lynn and Sandy Hook and, though it makes no sense, that tiny

lifeless body I held up to God during that awful day at Crawford Long Hospital.

And maybe that is as it should be. Pain and joy both occupy our hearts, and we cannot know one without having known the other.

This is frightening, if you give it much thought at all, because it affirms the truth that while this life is capable of handing us so much beauty, life is also capable of tearing our souls apart, leaving us to collect the remnants to try to piece together something whole again. And the truth is that we might fail in that effort.

There's no rhyme or reason to it—the heartache, the trauma, the awful days…and then the good and beautiful ones. Any attempt to imagine God's will moving celestial chess pieces such that a certain outcome will be achieved only leads to more heartache and a shallow sort of faith that declares some lives worth more than others.

Every life is sacred, and we live in a world that has forgotten this.

✌ ✌

One of my favorite Bible stories is Hagar and Ishmael. The way it's told, it's almost an aside, but it helps us understand the love of God for all of God's children so much more deeply.

Hagar, the handmaiden of a barren Sarah, is taken by Abraham so that he might have offspring (of course, in that day, preferably a son). She delivers him Ishmael.

Only after that is God's promise to Sarah that she would bear a child, too, made known, and Isaac, father of the twelve tribes of Israel, is born, to much rejoicing and thanksgiving.

Sarah casts Hagar aside as all this unfolds. It is not Sarah's finest moment, and her treatment of Hagar and Ishmael often gets overlooked when we tell the story of Isaac. But she casts them aside, not caring one whit what might happen to them.

But God remembers. Hagar calls upon God, and God remembers her and her son. God promises them their own descendants, their own lives to be lived, their own place as God's own.

I have often wondered if anyone besides that tiny baby's mother, the toddler sibling (if he was old enough to remember), and me remembers the baby I held in my hands that fall day at the hospital.

God remembers. I'm sure of it. Just as God remembers those lives ended far, far too soon at Sandy Hook, just as God holds close sweet Ruby's life, loving her and cheering her on, so grieves God the other lives lost, all lives lost.

～ ～

One summer evening—it must have been late summer, because the eggplant parmesan I was cooking for dinner had been made from homegrown vegetables and herbs, harvested just that afternoon from our backyard garden—company was coming for dinner, and I was in the last-minute-prep stages.

Dinner was five minutes from ready, the smell of the fresh tomatoes and just-picked basil and oregano in the sauce filling the kitchen. Bread bubbling with cheese and garlic was just out of the oven, the front porch table had been set, drinks served, and salad tossed.

"It's about ready!" I called out.

And then, Maddy's small sweet voice just behind me, "Mommy— where's my plate?"

"Right here, baby," I said, handing her a kid-sized plate of macaroni and cheese and apple slices. "Now go ahead and take it out to the table." And off she went, plate held carefully and head held high, and I turned to pull dinner from the oven.

I'd barely had time to deposit a hot casserole dish safely on a trivet when she returned, tears streaming down her face, "Mommy! There's nowhere for me to sit!"

I felt my face flame deep red as I realized the truth of her words. I'd left room for five at the table, but only set four places, intending to come back with her special cup and plate and a chair she'd be comfortable in. Only, in the rush to pull it all together, I'd forgotten, and, as a result, the little one in front of me clearly felt as if she, herself, had been forgotten.

And so it was with a quiet but insistent voice, and calm but sure movements that I turned to my little girl, looked into her brimming eyes, and assured her, "Oh honey, I'm so sorry. I didn't put your chair out. Come on—you can help me get it out there, and we'll get your very own place ready."

God does not forget. Not a single life. Each of us holds a place all our own in the heart of God, and it is in this truth that hope is to be found. Our lives do matter. *Every one.* Each one of us having been breathed into being by God and held close in God's heart from the first moment of our existence.

Chapter 3

SHIFT

I barely remember me before Maddy.

Events, sure. Special moments, yes. People and places I've loved, definitely. But any sense of self? Any clear idea of who I perceived myself to be? That's gone—I cannot grasp any solid memory of who I was without her.

Her dad and I had been married only a couple of years before we decided to "start trying" for a baby. It was a joyful decision, one that made us both walk around with goofy grins on our faces and inspired conversations about what the nursery would look like and what possible names might be. We were, as those hoping to be parents often are, simultaneously terrified and thrilled at the prospect of parenthood.

Almost a year into the trying, the joyful secret turned to private frustration and pain. My body was betraying me, failing to do what I had assumed it would and give us a baby. As it happens, I was not an immediate winner in the genetic lottery known as reproduction. I was referred to an infertility specialist with months of drug regimens, and conversations about diet and exercise. And monthly disappointments followed course.

I was not only profoundly disappointed personally; I felt as if I was actually a disappointment in general, especially to my husband,

who was never anything but supportive during those painful years. There's no logic to this, only the raw emotion of any woman struggling through the experience of infertility.

It sucks. And that's all there is to it.

I was only willing to go so far with fertility drugs. The medicine made me very sick and wreaked havoc with my emotions. Eventually we agreed, "No more drugs," and we began tentatively exploring adoption. Tentatively because my heart was too broken, my body too beat up and exhausted. Hope was hard to come by.

Late one summer, many months after we'd given up the fertility fight, another church—a bigger one than I was serving, in a large metropolitan area, one that could offer me a better compensation package—called and asked, "Would you consider being a candidate for us as we begin a search for a new youth minister?" We'd been contemplating a move for a while, and this seemed a great opportunity, and so I said yes, and a few months later the job was mine. Between Christmas and New Year's we picked up our lives and moved.

I resolved to "focus on my career." And I did my best to shelve the longing for a baby.

Essentially, we gave up—which, as many who have dealt with infertility know, is often the very thing that changes everything, because such is the way of the universe. And so six months later, just as I was preparing to leave for my first mission trip with a still-new-to-me group of high schoolers and still-learning-to-trust-me adult volunteers, I found myself walking into my new(ish) senior minister's office and saying, "I feel like I should tell you before I leave for this trip that I am about ten weeks pregnant." And then off I went to lead some twenty-five people through a week of serving and learning in one of the poorest counties in Eastern Kentucky—in the very heart of Appalachia.

Even though the trip was supposed to be a week, I made the decision to go home early. It had been, to say the least, a difficult three days. The fatigue and nausea coupled with the heat of a Kentucky summer were just too much.

That week was the first of many times I had to face the mighty change Maddy wrought in my life. That week, I experienced a visceral shift in my focus and attention, and it formed around the question, "Do I give everything I've got, even if it doesn't feel like much, to these kids? Or do I honor my body and my nurturing of this tiny life and go home?"

I chose the tiny life, for better or for worse. And I spent the next five years trying to work out what having chosen the tiny life meant for me and my career.

Every parent or caregiver I know struggles with his or her identity as that parent or caregiver and his or her otherwise personal and professional identity. Every parent or caregiver I know,

Maddy and me on Easter morning

especially those who work outside the home, wonders if he's getting the balance right. If she's managing to be her best at work and at home. If her children will suffer for her professional drive. If his children will feel neglected as he does his best to provide for them. It is generally assumed that this is especially true for mothers—but I see it in fathers, too.

I know many mothers and fathers and caregivers who can work with a kid right alongside, who navigate the office and the playroom

with a perceived ease that baffles me. I learned quickly I could not merge my identities as Reverend Youth Minister and Mommy successfully. The roles were too different, tapped different strengths in me, exhausted me in such different ways.

Perhaps it was because I felt so "on display." When you work in such a public realm and are privy to people's lives the way ministers are, it's difficult to carve out space of your own, difficult to allow yourself room to discern your way through a new landscape—in my case, motherhood—in a healthy way. In my efforts to prove I had it all handled, that I could balance being a perfect youth minister and a perfect mommy, I became so insecure at both that I second-guessed myself at every turn. And when you second-guess yourself, you become particularly vulnerable to the criticisms and directions of others, even if you know in the very core of your being that their criticisms, their directions, are wrong.

"Do you have Maddy on a schedule yet?" a church member and mother asked me, first thing, on my first Sunday back, post–maternity leave, "You know you need to have her on a schedule, right?" And I thought, then, "Omigod. I don't! What kind of mother am I?"

Now I would know what to tell her: "No, I don't. And that's because I do not myself, by virtue of my work, have a normal schedule. So why should I force her into one that doesn't work for either of us?"

One summer week, when Maddy was in preschool, I travelled out of the country with a fabulous group of teenagers, wanting so much to give myself to them 100 percent. But the first night I had to hang back at the edges of activity, fighting back tears at being so far away from my sweet girl, wondering how I'd ever get through the eight days without her. "You don't want to be here," an especially perceptive high school senior said, and I brushed away his concern, "No! I do! Very much! I'm just tired. I'll be fine tomorrow."

Now I'd tell him, "I do want to be here. Very much. But I also want to be with my daughter. Very much. And I don't know how

to reconcile those two things. I don't know how to do right by you all and her at the same time."

There are some days, now, several years and many experiences removed from those early days of Maddy and me, that I wish very much I could call those teenagers I worked with at the time all together and say, "I hope you know how much I loved you. How hard it was to eventually leave you. How thankful I am for the ways you made me the person I am. How sorry I am I wasn't better at sharing Maddy with you."

Everything I thought I knew about who I was and what I wanted from this life shifted the moment I knew she was coming.

She was in kindergarten when I decided it was time to "retire" from congregational youth ministry as a full-time occupation. I cannot pin it entirely on her. My own professional interests were changing, and I knew I could no longer do youth ministry the way the folks I served felt it needed to be done. This shift did not come easy, but, in the end, the best thing for everyone was for me to step back, focus on other ministry opportunities, and spend more time at home with Maddy.

"I don't know how this happened," my doctor had said, "but you are, indeed, pregnant." And then he'd added something I'll never forget, "Miracles do happen."

How could I now not give all of myself, with all my flaws and failings as a person, to this tiny miracle—proclaimed so by a medical professional? Easy decision, right?

Not by a long shot.

Walking away from fifteen years of congregational youth ministry felt like walking away from a piece of me, like I was leaving part of my heart in some past life that I'd never be able to get back to. I made the right decision, but it came at a cost of grief I didn't quite understand, sleepless nights, and many privately and publicly shed

tears. And it launched me into months, years, of wondering what in the world I was meant to do and be.

A few years ago, I woke in the wee hours of the morning feeling as if the entire ground had just moved underneath me. Indeed it had. An earthquake had rumbled through Kentucky, and for the first time, as the walls rattled and my heart rate bounced around wildly, I sensed what those who live with the daily threat of earthquakes must fear. It is profoundly unsettling to physically experience the ground shifting beneath you.

The world we live in, scary as it may be with its wars and bombs and guns and dead infants and heroin epidemics, is often at its scariest when something significant in our lives changes, when the known landscape of our existence cracks or crumbles and we are left staggering and stumbling.

Shifts happen.

And, when they do, it is sometimes all we can do to hold on while we ride out the transition, hoping that somewhere on the other side is waiting something solid, something worth landing on, something that we were meant for all along.

Meanwhile, we reach for what we know and trust. This is both good practice for ourselves and a wise thing to model for our children. Because, scheduled or not, their lives will change—likely more times than anyone will be entirely comfortable with—and how we navigate such change can make all the difference for how our children learn that navigation themselves.

My mother is a nurse. All my life she has worked full-time—in hospitals, as a home health nurse, in an IV therapy infusion suite, as a preventative care nurse. The context changed depending on where we were living or what our financial needs were as a family, but I've likely seen my mom in scrubs more than I have street clothes in my forty years. When I was in elementary school and Dad was just out of seminary and serving as a hospital chaplain

at Texas Children's Hospital in Houston, Mom worked nights in the ICU at nearby Methodist Hospital. She slept while Joy and I were at school, but during the summer we'd be home as she slept in preparation for her night shift.

Sometimes now, when Dad and Mom and Joy and I are all together, telling family stories, and Mom doesn't remember something, she'll say, "Oh—maybe I was asleep," with more than a bit of self-deprecation, even as she tries to pass it off as a joke. Once I heard her add, "I sometimes feel as if I slept through most of your childhood."

Mom vs. Nurse Jeannine. I had no way of understanding then what a struggle that must have been for her. I do now. What I also know is this: her life is proof positive it is possible to live your professional calling and your role as a mother with tremendous grace and grit on both fronts.

What I've come to believe is that we talk a whole lot about, in these privileged United States, the balance of work and life: "quality parenting time" and our professional identities. And we talk about it as if these parts of ourselves exist in total dichotomy.

This is ridiculous, as is anytime we try to compartmentalize one part of our lives, our hearts, our brains, or our souls from another part. The disaster of our Puritan ancestors' attempts to separate the needs of the body and the needs of the soul should have taught us this. And, yet...

We are not meant to live in isolation, from one another or from ourselves, and this is perhaps no more important than when it comes to how we model life and well-being for children. Maddy needs all of me to be her mother—not just the parts I've reserved as the ones I've deemed most fitting for a mother-daughter relationship.

How else will she learn to embrace her full self unless her parents model it for her?

How else will she learn to care unless she sees her father going to pray with someone at the hospital or tags along when he marches in the community Martin Luther King Jr. memorial parade every year? Or when she comes with me to deliver clothes or food to a local shelter? How else will she learn a strong work ethic if the adults in her life don't model that for her? How else will she learn that having been born a girl does not demand that she conform to all pink and all dolls and all Easy Bake ovens unless she is shown that such stereotypes are meant to be shattered?

I speak from my own context as mother and minister. But this battle, this desire to find some sense of balance to it all, it is not just mine. It is not just a mother's. It is not just a minister's.

I wonder if maybe the real thing we search for as our lives shift and shift again is wholeness. A way of being all we're called to be, such that we're able to live honestly and boldly and with all our hopes and dreams tied up in the day-to-day of carpools and homework and work meetings, and tight household budgets and the evening news reminding us how terrifying it is to face each day—all this with some sense that all is not lost, that it will all be okay, somehow.

Even when shifts happen.

And I wonder if maybe the way to the wholeness we crave is to be found in what most grounds us—what makes us feel safe, connected. As if we are exactly where we're meant to be in that particular moment.

After his time as a chaplain in Houston, Dad was called to pastor a small church in Bay City, Texas—Matagorda County, some twenty miles from local Gulf Coast beach access. My mom worked first at the local hospital when we moved to Bay City, and then as a home health care nurse in a neighboring county. During the years we lived there, for a week every summer, I went to church camp at Camp Wildur, a swampy, densely wooded stretch in southeast Texas.

The summer after my fourth grade year, Dad served as the director for the week I was at camp. As I remember it, his cabin was on the opposite side of the tennis courts and swimming pool from a line of cabins where I stayed. Each cabin had four or five bunk beds and housed up to ten kids for a week of camp.

Early in the week that camp session, sometime during the night, I woke up. I had no clear idea what time it was or where I was. I looked around and saw surroundings that seemed familiar, including broad wooden support beams encasing an attic fan doing its best to offer some relief from the oppressive humidity of south Texas in July. As sleep fell away further, I pushed myself up on one arm and became aware I was perched on the top of a wooden set of bunk beds, also familiar, since I could remember falling asleep on top of such a bunk.

But something felt very, very wrong. My heart began to race with nine-year-old anxiety as I tried to figure out exactly what. And then, suddenly, the vinyl mattress beneath me began helping my brain process what it hadn't been able to work through—the mattress should have been covered with my old cotton sleeping bag. The other bunk beds, barely discernible shadows through the darkness but clearly empty, should have been occupied by my campmates. An open door should have been firmly shut and latched. And then what was wrong became abundantly and frightfully clear. I was alone, with no idea how I'd gotten where I was or where in the world my cabin counselors and the other girls I was living with for the week could possibly have gone.

I vaguely remember the pure panic that immediately claimed me, my body tensing with fear, breath quickly turning shallow and mind racing with wild imaginings. Frozen on the outside, scrambling with utter terror on the inside, I sat exactly where I was, unable to speak or move. And just then—just when I thought I couldn't possibly take it anymore—a large shadow loomed outside, and I heard footsteps land on the cabin's threshold. And then Dad's

strong arms pulled me off that top bunk and into the tight safety of his embrace. He carried me outside into wee-hour darkness and gently deposited me onto a camp sidewalk that linked all the girls' cabins together. I distinctly remember seeing, as we walked, out of the corner of my eye, the silver flash of an armadillo nuzzling for food along the ground.

Soon Dad lifted me in his arms again, only this time slipping me safely into my sleeping bag, in my own bed, in my own cabin, brushing a kiss across my forehead. In the background the form of my clearly relieved cabin counselor stood quietly, murmuring her sighs of thanksgiving as Dad scooted out the door.

The next morning over breakfast the whole story was pieced together—how Pat, my counselor, had woken up in the night to find me banging against the screen window of the cabin's back wall, how she'd tried to steer me to bed and then found me again, a few minutes later, up and begging to go to the bathroom. Pat let me out the door of the cabin, sure I could handle the very few steps between the cabin and the girls' bathhouse.

Normally, she'd have been right, but Pat had no way of knowing I was actually sleepwalking, completely unaware of my words, actions or movement. Against her own will, tired as all camp counselors are at night, she fell asleep almost as soon as I left, and didn't wake up until a good bit later. I was long gone by then, having walked, deeply asleep, to an empty cabin several doors down, crawled up on a bunk corresponding to mine in location, and curled up, still sleeping.

I cannot imagine how Pat must have felt having to go banging on the camp director's door in the middle of the night to say, "John, I'm so sorry—I can't find Julie and I need help." A difficult admission for anyone to make, perhaps much more so when the child you've lost is said director's own child. For years after that, my church camp and mission trip and school field trip permission forms always

indicated under the "Special Needs" column: "Avid sleepwalker, please watch out for her at night and lock door to room."

Over the years I shared the story as a cautionary tale to fellow camp counselors and youth sponsors. And, every time, I thought, "How scared Dad must have been when Pat came knocking on his door!"

I only fully understood that fear once Maddy arrived.

But here's the thing: what I remember most about that night, beyond the fear, is that eventually, before I even had time to panic, I was held safe. Protected. Grounded in the strength of having been found.

How do we, when we feel ungrounded, when we feel all that we know shifting around and beneath us, when things don't seem quite right, find something to anchor us? When work or relationships or our own private thoughts keep us from offering our best selves to our children, how do we find firm footing again? What makes us feel held safe? What keeps us confident that we are not alone in the struggle?

Our children need us to be able to answer these questions. Need to know that we're working towards wholeness. Need to believe that they themselves are part of our own journey to getting there.

They need us to hold them safe while they seek such wholeness themselves.

Despite the shifts along the way.

Chapter 4

SKIN

The summer after my sophomore year of college I found myself not wanting to head home to Winder for the summer and also not wanting to stay in college-town Rome, Georgia. Also, I needed a job.

The church camp where I'd spent a good bit of my summers growing up was looking for an assistant cook in the camp kitchen. "Assistant Cook" really meant "Assistant to Cleo"—the aging woman from south Georgia who'd been serving up three meals a day to church camp kids for more summers than any of us really knew for sure.

Cleo had shoulder-length, thick gray hair. She often wore it down, held loosely off her forehead with two barrettes, and she wore long pants and almost always long sleeves. The kitchen we worked in was so hot that I often wondered how she endured it, with so much covering her up. Cleo was a legend, and deservedly so. She made the best peanut butter cookies in the entire southeastern United States. When the camp menu called for a baked potato bar, she'd spend the morning frying up bacon for those potatoes—no fake bacon chips for her kids, thank you very much. She believed in the liberal use of pure lard in her cooking, and she once taught me the culinary bliss of a sweet Vidalia onion slow-cooked in butter, brown sugar, and Worcestershire sauce until it fell apart into bite-sized pieces of heaven.

Cleo was getting too old to lift big pans of potatoes from the oven, or pull down multi-pound boxes of biscuit mix from the upper shelves of the pantry. She could still cook, but the physical requirements of the job were becoming a challenge. I loved Cleo, and so when the powers that be asked me if I wanted to work with her, I enthusiastically said yes, eager to spend a summer at a beloved place, doing the heavy lifting and cleaning so Cleo so could keep working her magic.

Gordon, Georgia, isn't much more than a wide spot on the road between Macon and Milledgeville. That it exists at all is largely because of a kaolin plant located there. Middle Georgia has several of these plants, where the white clay mineral called kaolin is mined. Kaolin is used in all sorts of white china and/or porcelain, so it's likely if you've got some kind of porcelain figurine perched on your fireplace mantle or in your grandmother's china cabinet, you know kaolin, even if you didn't realize it. Drive off-road a bit in the middle part of Georgia, and you find pits of it, where white mud crusts along the bottom of a Jeep worse than any of that red clay Georgia's known for. Kaolin aside, Gordon, Georgia is, more importantly, at least in my life, home to Camp Christian.

I've not been to Camp Christian, to Gordon, in well over a decade, but I can tell you what the dense humidity of a warm August morning rolling off the lake looks like. And if I close my eyes and call up the memories of those summer nights, I hear the cicadas calling to one another after dusk falls over the pine trees.

I showed up at camp the first week of June, ready for a summer of mostly white middle-class church kids doing their camp thing while Cleo and I kept them fed. What I didn't know is that there'd been a new addition to the camp schedule, a week of camp for children enrolled in a program called AIM (Aid to Imprisoned Mothers).[1] Camp AIM was the brainchild of AIM's founder, an

---

[1] AIM is now known as Forever Family, and is still headquartered in Atlanta.

Atlanta-based attorney who was also a member of a large African American congregation in Atlanta called Ray of Hope.

The children coming to Camp AIM were children of mothers who were imprisoned in the metro-Atlanta area. AIM's work was to keep those children in relationship with their moms despite the distance created by prison walls. I remember some forty kids at the camp. There were also several counselors, handpicked by AIM's founder, all students at either Spelman College or Morehouse College, Atlanta's prestigious and historically black colleges.

That week at Camp Christian, Cleo and I were the only residents with white skin. And while I was certainly no stranger to being around folks with a different skin color than me, it was a first for me to be in such stark minority for such an extended period of time. This dynamic alone made the week a very different sort of experience.

For whatever reason, by the evening of the first day, one of the Morehouse students and I had forged a connection. Marketus didn't just have brown skin—he had the darkest skin you can imagine, and next to my whiter-than-your-average-white complexion, it looked even darker. And the vivid visual contrast was not the only difference between us. He was a city kid, raised with his twin brother by a single mom, and he had seen some of the worst of what Atlanta's tougher neighborhoods can offer up—drugs, gangs, gun violence. And though bucolic Berry College and urban Morehouse are not even 100 miles apart, their cultures, landscapes, and populations were (and probably still are) vastly different.

Still, Marketus and I enjoyed each other's company, and in those first few days we spent a good bit of time together when I wasn't cooking or cleaning and he wasn't surrounded by energetic elementary-aged boys.

One night, about three days or so into camp, with campers in bed and both of us restless, Marketus and I were sitting up in the

camp kitchen. As our walk-in cooler had gone on the fritz just before dinner, a local electrician was making a late-night service call to camp. Marketus kept me company while I waited up for the guy to finish his job, Cleo having gone on to bed much earlier. At some point, the electrician broke through our conversation and mumbled something about having done what he could, but he wasn't sure it would last. And then, words that knifed into my very being: "This damn fridge is so nigger-rigged, I'm not even sure what to do with it!"

I froze, jaw dropped and breath suspended, afraid to meet Marketus' eyes, my cheeks flooding red with horror at the words I'd just heard. I reached out a hand, grabbed his arm, tried to apologize—"It's okay," Marketus said, "Don't worry about it."

The electrician left soon—not soon enough—frustrated and still cursing the uncooperative refrigerator, and Marketus and I both headed in for the night, not another word exchanged about what we'd heard and experienced. I did not sleep well.

The electrician failed in a number of ways that evening, the least of which being that the cooler died overnight. The next morning, our milk supply soured, Cleo sent me into town to pick up enough milk to last through breakfast. On my way down the dirt road leaving camp, Marketus flagged me to a stop and asked if I wanted company for the ride. I readily opened the door to him, thankful the events of the night before hadn't caused an irreparable rift, and we chatted easily on the way to the Piggly Wiggly.

Quickly, knowing starving elementary students would soon descend upon the camp dining hall, we ran into the store, bee-lining toward the dairy aisle. As we approached yellow gallons of Mayfield milk, I realized Marketus' steps had slowed, and I looked up just in time to register what he was seeing: an entire grocery store of the white residents of Gordon staring unabashedly at Marketus and me, some turning away with disapproving stares, some daring to point directly at us. While Marketus was, near as I could tell, the

only black person in the store, I have always assumed the real crime we committed was being together—a white girl and a black boy.

The same mortification that had overwhelmed me at the electrician's ugly words the night before came rushing back. I could not grab the needed gallons of milk and get out the door fast enough. I could not look Marketus in the eye. I could not speak a word to him. I was so, so painfully embarrassed.

Things did not go well for Marketus and me after that. We tried to talk about it, but I found his righteous anger too daunting, and he found my stunned disbelief too much to conquer. We got through the week, exchanged a few letters that pretended the incident had never happened once we both got back to our respective schools, but eventually lost touch somewhere around the holidays that year.

Years later, social media having been born, Marketus and I connected on Facebook. We'd both finished graduate degrees by that time and were well into postsecondary education life. And we'd both grown up enough to be able to have a conversation—as much as one can have one over Facebook messaging—about that summer in Gordon. Neither one of us had had the vocabulary or self-awareness at age nineteen to talk about race and relationship, but in our early thirties we were both able to offer apologies for the demise of what could have been a lovely friendship. "It would have been too hard back then," we both said, in one way or another, the admission stinging in its truth.

And it would have been.

We do a pretty rotten job of fostering healthy conversations about race in our country. Perhaps our fear of offending stymies our desire for asking honest questions and seeking honest answers. Perhaps we just don't know how to work past hundreds of years of conflict and oppression. Perhaps we are so aware of the challenges we still have in this area we aren't even sure where to begin. Whatever the reason, it seems no surprise that two teenagers couldn't have a real and helpful conversation when very few grown and mature adults can.

For a long while I hadn't thought about Marketus. That changed the day my daughter came home from her first day of first grade. She had begun a new school, a public, magnet school for the performing arts right in the middle of downtown Louisville drawing students from all across Jefferson County, a far cry from the very small and very safe and very familiar private preschool and kindergarten she'd gone to. In her first grade class alone were at least ten different ethnicities, plus multiple native languages.

We were celebrating a successful first day over ice cream, me extracting what bits of information I could from her between bites of Cookies n' Cream, and I asked, "Hey, what was lunch like, sweetie? Did you eat with your class?"

"Oh, yes. We all sat together."

"Well, what did the cafeteria serve?" She'd packed lunch for her first day, wary of any school menu, and I'd told her if what she saw in the cafeteria looked good, she could take or buy either way. The choice was hers.

"I'm not sure," she replied, "I think I saw a biscuit or a bun or something. It smelled good though!"

Laughing, I said, "Well, that's good!"

Then, after a long pause and some very methodical licks of her ice cream cone, she said, "But, Mommy? Mostly it was brown-skinned kids who bought their lunch. Everyone else brought their own. All the kids like me—we had lunch boxes."

I didn't say anything for a moment. Speechless at her observation. Finally I managed a rather pathetic, "Really?"

Her response came fast and certain, "Yes. It was mostly the brown-skinned kids. And I thought, you know, maybe, Mommy, the brown-skinned kids don't have lunch boxes. Do you think they do, Mommy?"

"I don't know...."

My "I don't know" was an equivocation the likes of which only a parent desperate for the right words yet unable to find them can make. We all do it. Our children ask these very profound and unpredictable questions, and we stall for time while we scramble to organize our thoughts into some semblance of truth-but-not-quite-truth.

Because, how do you talk to a six-year-old about race and socioeconomics in the nation's sixteenth largest city, where a clear divide between white and black exists at 9th Street downtown, and where for years immigrants have adopted many neighborhoods around town—yet somehow we're all struggling to figure out how to coexist?

How do you talk to a six-year-old about free lunch programs, and Title I funding, and diversity quotas in the public school system?

How do you talk to a six-year-old about her own innate white privilege, especially when what you want for her is not to feel guilty or judged by the privilege but to honor it as a means to help those who do not have such privilege?

If Marketus and I, just the two of us, sitting on a swing by a lake in the Georgia woods, could not have an honest conversation about these things, about the truths of all that made us different from one another, how was I to find the words to answer my daughter's very astute observation of a system bigger than any of us, but in which we all play a part?

In the simplest language I could that day, I talked to Maddy, trusting that if she was asking such questions it was okay to try to answer them, about how people with brown skin and people with white skin have often had a hard time figuring out how to be together. I had no idea how to actually address the issue of brown-skinned kids and lunch boxes, but I reminded her of things her dad and I both have told her before—that the color of a person's skin does not matter, is

completely irrelevant. That it is what a person's insides are like that we should pay attention to—how they act and think and feel. And I told her that in lots of places, including where we live, there are many brown-skinned people who have a hard time making it.

I told her about slavery. This she could not fathom. And I told her that not so long ago in this country people with brown skin and people with white skin couldn't go to school together. This did not set well at all.

"*What?!?*" was her fierce response. "You mean Chernet and I couldn't have gone to the same school? You mean we could not have been friends? You mean…?" And on she went.

Maddy's father, having travelled to Palestine and studied long and hard the conflict between the people of Palestine and (it sometimes seems) the rest of the world, is a tireless advocate for people of Arab and Muslim descent. Maddy's maternal grandfather has spent a great deal of his life involved in race relations, especially as this pertains to black folks and white folks in the South. This is, no doubt, at least in part because he is a graduate of Central High School in Little Rock, Arkansas, where in 1957 nine black students enrolled and were denied entrance to the segregated school by their state's Governor Faubus, and so ensued a stand-off between Faubus and his supporters and President Eisenhower. And, her maternal great-grandfather once risked his standing and relationships with friends and business associates because he, an accomplished song leader in the *a capella* Churches of Christ, insisted on leading music at a black church in Little Rock, Arkansas. He did this during the summers of 1958 and 1959—a time when such things were decidedly *not* done. And her mother holds close the stories of Marketus and of a little boy named Adam (his story is held in these pages, too) as stories of what it means to see beyond skin color and into a person's heart.

All this—such questions, such desire to make right the injustices of the world based on skin color—is to say, *It is in her blood.* And,

with her one simple question about lunch boxes and lunch lines, and without even realizing what she'd done, Maddy joined us in the fight.[2]

"Jesus loves the little children," she was taught in the church nursery, "all the children of the world, red and yellow, black and white, they are precious in his sight...."

In Jesus' sight, perhaps, but not so much always in ours.

Black, yellow, red, and white, our sight is clouded—by politics and economics, by misunderstanding and fear, by a media who, sometimes unconsciously and sometimes purposefully, propagates those emotions. Our sight is clouded by our own ignorance and unknowing. Our sight is clouded by our fear and judgment. Our sight is clouded by hundreds of years of history that we continue to let define us in the worst ways possible, instead of using it as a way to move forward, away from division and into life together.

"You can't possibly understand!" Marketus yelled at me that day on the way home from the Gordon Piggly Wiggly.

"We're not all like that!" I protested through tears.

He was right. I couldn't possibly understand. And I was right. White people are not "all like that." But even us both being right couldn't move us past the moment. And so, is it any wonder that in the United States of America we cannot find our way past the collective moments in which we, as a people, have failed to recognize all that we have in common as human beings? As children of God?

Maddy's sight is not clouded. Nor is the sight of most children. Unless they have been taught that someone with a certain skin color

---

[2]Since this conversation, Maddy has been given, and has read, Brad Meltzer's *I Am Rosa Parks* (New York: Dial Books, 2014) and Robert Coles's *The Story of Ruby Bridges* (New York: Scholastic, 1995). I heartily recommend both to parents wanting to talk to their children about the history of race in the United States. Ms. Parks and Ms. Bridges are two of Maddy's "she-roes" now.

is the enemy, they do not care one whit. They know what Jesus meant. They see God in one another. They live and play together, as things were meant to be—not as our world has too often made it.

While we moan and wail and fight and destroy and breed judgment and foster hatred,...they love. Without question. Without condition. As fully as their gorgeous hearts are able.

Most days, I find myself wondering when we will understand this, wondering when we will begin to listen to all that they could teach us. Hate clamors. Systemic racism strangles. Mistrust breeds contempt. And so the battle rages on, our collective history of white privilege and black oppression something we adults just cannot seem to shake. And I feel this must break God's heart.

It's on us, entirely. Us grown-ups, that is. Our children are not born with the prejudices we develop over time, try as we might to escape them. They must be taught that which divides them from those who are different. And we teach them, in a thousand ways every day, implicitly and explicitly, consciously and unconsciously.

When will we stop writing such lessons, and begin instead to learn what it means that all have been made precious in God's sight?

Chapter 5

PLAYGROUND

I was somewhere around the age of ten when I first heard someone described as "gay." I had been privy to some after-dinner adult conversation that perhaps would not have happened if my quiet presence (reading in the living room corner) had been obvious, but it did, and so later I asked, "Daddy, what does that mean?" He told me. And I said, "Oh, well, I don't know anybody like that."

I've never forgotten his response.

"Yes. Yes you do, Julie. You just don't know it."

"Oh," I said. And Dad left me to ponder what he'd said, and my inability to respond to it, for the next several years.

I was sixteen when I first heard someone whisper, "He's...*like that,*" about my friend Rick. Rick and I went to the same church—and he was a favored counselor at summer church camp and also my favorite duet partner in the church choir. I never heard anyone actually say, "Rick's gay," as if the word *gay* itself was too taboo to speak aloud, but the inferences of ,"He's different," or, "Of *course* he's a theatre buff," were all too clear the older I got.

I was a college freshman when one of my roommates and her girlfriend were bullied so badly by a group of self-proclaimed Christians for being lesbian that they both transferred out and

away before Christmas of our sophomore year. Ill-concealed whispers in the dining hall,…pointing fingers,…Bible verses taped surreptitiously to their dorm doors,…words like "dyke" and "butch" thrown around by voices thick with judgment. I never saw or heard anything about either of them again.

I was in my first year of seminary when University of Wyoming student Matthew Shepard[1] was tortured and beaten, tied to fence rail outside Laramie, and left to die. I remember a very visceral reaction to this event: this feeling that all I'd heard or seen before in terms of exclusion or fear of LGBT persons was nothing compared to such blatant contempt for human life. And still, when I think of him, strapped to that fence all night long, life fading out of him, my heart twists into such grief over what we human beings are capable of doing to one another.

I was married with a full-time job and a toddler when a family member called to tell me, "You know I'm gay, right? I just needed to tell you. I know you're okay with it." "Of course I am," I said, wishing I could reach through the phone lines and pull him into a supportive embrace, adding, "I love you."

I was a dozen years into congregational ministry when, following a Sunday morning worship service in which some particularly passionate and outspoken youth had made clear their belief that "God loves LGBT[2] people, too," I was told that my allowing such a display of their convictions had led to the departure of a family from the church—and that, despite many accolades from other church members over the graciousness and bold faith of our youth, I needed to remember, "Not everyone agrees with you on this," and was admonished to "be more careful" next time. It was not the

---

[1]If you are not familiar with Matthew's story, please visit the Matthew Shepard Foundation website, www.matthewshepard.org.

[2]I know that the acronym LGBT (Lesbian, Gay, Bisexual, Transgender) will not suffice for some readers. And I know that for others it may be off-putting. But it is the best term I know to use out of my own experience with persons who identify as lesbian, gay, bisexual, or transgender. It is my intent to cast the net as wide as possible. If I have failed in that, it is only because of my own inability to fully understand the identity issues at stake.

first time I felt admonished by a congregation to keep my mouth shut about my opinions on LGBT.

When I served in congregational ministry, I never felt I could truly declare myself for what I had become—an LGBT ally. I never felt I could say what I believe: that I do not understand it, but I don't need to. God created LGBT persons I know and love just as they are, and God loves them fiercely, just as they are. And my job is to do the same, no questions, exclusions, or qualifications necessary. I wish very much that I had stopped "being careful," long before I did. I wish I'd had the guts in my mid-twenties to say, "No. This is wrong. And if we are not going to claim these men and women as our full brothers and sisters in faith, and welcome them as we have been welcomed, then I want no part of what we are calling 'church.'"

I have long believed homophobia and the fear and hatred of the transgendered is the last socially acceptable prejudice in the United States, just as racism was socially acceptable until the civil rights movement exposed it for the pure evil it is.

It's still "okay" to not be okay with members of the LGBT community. It's still "okay" to "love the sinner, hate the sin" (I cannot even tell you how ridiculous and offensive and *un*-loving I find that phrase). It's still "okay" to stand against the full acceptance and inclusion of LGBT folks for "religious reasons." We once defended slavery, gender inequality, and marriage for property reasons "because the Bible says so." But when's the last time you heard someone defending slavery in public? Or *openly* professing sexism as a good business model or productive societal value? Sexism exists and so does racism, and each "ism" rips at the fabric of our society with such bitter destruction. But anyone idiotic enough to publicly defend racism or sexism will usually draw harsh critique and righteous anger. Sexism is subtle. Systemic. So is racism. But in the United States, you can't get away with either one in the public for very long.

Homophobia, though? The exclusion or condemnation of transgender individuals? You can get away with that. Especially if you happen to fall into a particular brand of Christianity that blames hatred and prejudice on "what God wants." As I write these words in the months following the Supreme Court's ruling that allows same-sex marriage nationwide, this all remains true, even as baby steps forward are made in our legal system and people's hearts. Maybe you are reading this book in a world in which the tide has magnificently and finally shifted. I'm hopeful. Sort of.

But, meanwhile, statistics of homelessness, anxiety, depression, and suicide remain startlingly high for LGBT youth. And there are churches still raving stark mad about how "traditional American values" are under attack. And in very public places LGBT folks are often still judged, maligned, and made to feel less-than. And again and again phrases such as "moral values" and "religious principles" get thrown up as defense for what boils down to a judgment born of fear and ignorance.

While I was writing this book, a dear friend and trusted colleague, who is also a gay man, called. He had just passed through Lexington and Louisville, and so I'd seen him recently, and thought maybe he was just checking in on the ride home.

I was wrong. He was calling to tell me about what had happened when he made a coffee stop at a fast-food joint. Standing in line for coffee and a biscuit, he'd suddenly found himself the subject of hostile stares and an obvious effort on the part of others to steer clear of him. One man in particular intentionally drew the lines of people at the counter into a wide berth around my friend. As my friend wondered what in the world was going on, he realized he was wearing a T-shirt from his hometown's annual Gay Pride event.

As the realization of what was happening sunk in, as he processed that these people didn't want to be around him because of who they assumed him to be, "I felt physically ill," he told me. I hung up the phone after we'd finished talking, I pulled to the side of the

road, and I cried—because *no one,* in any moment, for any reason, should be made to feel so very "other" than those around them.

You know what Maddy thinks of this whole LGBT issue?

Nothing. Absolutely nothing.

You know why? Because, since the day she was born, she has been surrounded by people of all walks of life and lifestyle. Because, in her preschool class, Ethan had two mommies, and in her second-grade class, Grant had two mommies, and her friend Rachel's dad dates men. She has never known anything different. It is a non-issue for her.

I realized the full impact of this aspect of her life one summer Saturday, as I sat on a playground bench watching Maddy play with a kid she knows from school. Maddy has gone to school with this particular child for several years, since they were just wee preschool kiddos, long before they landed at the same elementary school. They have lots of the same friends and so they have seen each other off and on outside of school several times, too.

When they were in preschool, the child was known by a girl's name. Now the child identifies as male. I first learned this because (1) parents talk in the carpool line, "They've had a hard time... It's been a really difficult journey," and (2) I have eyes that can see the change. Typical boys' clothing and shoes. Typical boys' haircut. Typical everything boy. And Michelle is now Michael.

This child has amazing and brave family and other allies in his life helping him along as he navigates things. I suspect he has experienced just the opposite, too, and so I pray for his parents, for all those who know and love him best, knowing that this world will sometimes be cruel to their precious one.

He and Maddy played with the carefree Saturday morning joy of any happy and cared-for child that day, racing up the jungle gym and taunting each other across the monkey bars and seeing who

could get down the slide the fastest. And his mom and I watched. And laughed. As all parents do at their children's playground antics.

Eventually the conversation turned to, "So how's the school year going?" And, as we answered that shared question, I learned we were both in the midst of a divorce. I learned, too, that the school our children attends has risen to the occasion of nurturing and loving Maddy's friend through his transition, just as they loved Maddy through her learning to be the child of divorced parents.

"You know he's...transgender?" his mom asked me, the merest hesitation making it obvious that she still isn't always sure her son will be safe in any given environment, even with parents she may have reason to trust. "I do," I said, "and I'm really glad he has had so much support at school." She nodded her head, smiled, and said, with so much love and so much of what I can only describe as parental angst heavy in her voice, "Yeah. Me, too."

On the way home that day, Maddy said, out of the blue, "You know, Mommy, last year, Michael went to the girls' bathroom. This year, he goes to the boys' bathroom."

I took a deep breath and I said, "Really?" "Yep!" she chirped from the backseat, and so I prodded some more, "Do you need to talk about that?"

"Nope," was her definitive response, "He's just my friend."

That's it. Easy-peasy-lemon-squeezy, as she and I say about any simply solved situation.

He's just my friend.

For the love, y'all, when will we get this? What will it take so that we can stop with the fear-mongering, the ignorance, the insistence that everyone must be like us or they do not count? When will we stop with the name-calling, the judgment, and simply let one another be?

My small-town high school produced many a gay, lesbian, bisexual, or transgender student. But I didn't know it until years later. And if I suspected it, well, it wasn't something we talked about. It was too hard. Our playground was rife with prejudice of all kinds. How any of us survived it often seems a small miracle to me.

A couple of years ago, I had the opportunity to catch up with such a friend from high school. He's a wildly successful attorney, and he and his husband have the unequivocal support of family and friends as they build their life together. We talked nonstop over lunch about people we'd both known, and experiences we both remembered, and where our lives had taken us since we graced the hallways of Winder-Barrow High School.

And I wanted so much to ask, "Did we make it hard for you? Were we unknowingly cruel? Did we make you feel less than the beautiful human being you are?" Because, here in front of me, sat this incredible man, confident and gracious, and if we'd made his journey to being whole more difficult, even if we hadn't realized it, I wanted to apologize. For all of us. Even if not all of us would be willing to apologize.

These days, I am convinced Maddy and her friends are our greatest helpers in helping us older folks see the LGBT community with loving and welcoming eyes instead of fearful and distant ones. I am convinced they are the ones we should look to for a new way of living life together, positive that she and her playground peers have everything they need to show us the way to real acceptance.

I am also convinced the tide is turning, albeit far too slowly for some of us. Even more, though, I'm reminded again that fear and hate—these things must be *taught*; they are not inherent to our nature as human beings. Whether we're discussing race, immigration, religion, or LGBT folks, whatever the "other of the day" might be—kids learn to fear and hate by watching the people they admire or respect practice fear and hate. Hate and exclusion are taught by those who *want* their children to carry on a mantle of

hate and exclusion, thereby reducing their children to foot soldiers in their own personal wars of fear and ignorance.

Our lives are too short for such misguided education. Our world too beautiful in its diversity. Our children too lovely in their care for one another. Our lives already complicated enough.

~ ~

In this LGBT conversation, there is another issue, one that often gets pushed aside. It is one that concerns me deeply when it comes to our children and their understanding of being whole and beloved.

Inherent in the back-and-forth, in the judgment and assumption and fear, is this idea that our sexual identity is our *only* identity. More books than I could list here, more study than I could ever do, and more solid theological, social, and psychological research than I could cite have been done about sexual identity—healthy or unhealthy, gay or straight, abusive or consensual. I do not have enough empirical or experiential knowledge to add to any of this research or conversation or writing.

What I can do is acknowledge this: We have a very difficult time talking about sex in healthy ways in the United States. We have an especially hard time talking about in our communities of faith. And we have an exceptionally hard time talking about it with our kids.

But, if we don't talk about it, if we don't make an effort to help our children understand that God made them to be in relationship, made them to enjoy healthy and consensual sexual relationships, made them to feel the things they feel physically as they grow and change and develop—if we can't find a way to talk about these things in ways that do not define, but educate and empower, then we are potentially setting our children on the most dangerous of courses.

Despite any blushing and protestations and embarrassment— often more on our part than theirs— our kids are starving to

have honest conversations about sex. Hungry for someone trusted to talk to about the crazy things their bodies put them through in adolescence; dying to know how to handle deep physical attraction; desperate, even if they don't know it, for solid physical and emotional boundaries that will see them safely through to adulthood.

How they need us to help them see they are so much more than their physical selves! And how they also need us to talk to them about how to manage their physical selves.

And how, especially, do our LGBT children, who have been dealt a double whammy when it comes to emerging sexuality, need us to say, "It's okay. And I love you. And I'll walk with you while you figure this out."

~ ~

Once, years ago, my friend Mark said to me, "You know, Julie, I don't need to be your cause. I just need to know you love me. And that you'll speak up for me if necessary."

He spoke such gospel truth. Causes fade. People lose interest. And, sooner or later, another more popular, sexier cause will come along. But since the dawn of time until its evening, whenever that comes, there will be LGBT persons in this world we live in, and such persons are not causes to be claimed, but human beings to be embraced for all that they are, as each of us has been embraced by the One who knows and loves us best.

I have grown so weary of theological and/or philosophical debates over LGBT persons. I often refuse to engage in scriptural battles over "what the Bible says" anymore. Bottom line, I believe the entire, overarching message of God to be one of unconditional and all-encompassing love, and any way of interpreting the scriptures of my faith tradition that fails to exhibit that unconditional and all-encompassing love is not a way of understanding God that I have any interest in—nothing in the stories I know from scripture

tells me anything but that God is love. Period. Those who disagree with me on that point understand the Bible and who God is in such a vastly different way, it is difficult to even find a starting point for discussion.

Still, there's so much hurt that has come from exclusive ways of interpreting Christian scripture, and I cannot, because of this, disengage entirely.

It would be far easier if I could tell you of some *aha!* moment, some Saul-to-Paul story of how I came to be an LGBT ally. But I can't. Because, for me, it has been an entire lifetime of being taught, by my parents, by theological study, and by life experience that God's love is so much bigger, so much wider, so much more vast than we could ever understand—and in this love is room enough for all God's people.

This is precisely why Mark...Rick...Matthew...my other friends and family members and ones I'll one day know...they are not "causes." They are human beings, part of my journey through this life, and no more whole or broken than me. Different than me in very crucial ways, sure, but in so many more ways, and especially in God's unconditional love for us, so very much the same.

Chapter 6

SHELTER

I've lived in Kentucky for some fifteen years, and I learned early on that weather in central Kentucky and the broader Ohio Valley can get pretty sketchy from about late April to early September. During these months, the air often feels unsettled and heavy, and crazy-loud, driving rain and bright lightning storms are to be expected. I have, more than once, as most folks in such parts have, been caught in such storms while driving, knuckles white from clenching the steering wheel, emergency lights on, and every breath a prayer for a safe arrival home.

Memorial Day weekend, 2004, I got caught in such a storm. My seminary classmate Erin was being ordained in London, Kentucky, an hour or so south of Lexington, and I had a role in the ordination service. While we were all eating cake and punch in the church fellowship hall after the service, warnings started popping up on the church's weather radio and people started getting phone calls about weather in the area. A line of severe thunderstorms with "tornadic activity" were tracking toward Lexington.

I remember making a very fast (and, as it turns out, less than wise) decision to leave immediately for my drive home to Midway, just northwest of Lexington. "I'll be fine," I insisted, over numerous protests from colleagues and friends, all extra-worried because they

knew I'd be driving alone, "but I need to go now and try to get home before it hits."

I couldn't have been more than twenty minutes into my hour drive home, straight up a congested yet fast-moving (even more so than usual, especially given the weather) I-75 northbound, when the skies began a dance of vengeance. Rain so heavy my windshield wipers could not keep up. Wind so powerful I fought to keep my Toyota RAV4 on the road. Thunder so loud I could hardly hear myself think. Jagged lightning stabbing at the earth over and over.

I had the Lexington public radio station on, and though its reception was compromised by the storm, I could hear enough to know that I was in dangerous territory—the phrase, "tornado warning" twisting a hard knot in my stomach. I pulled out my cell, not a decision I'd usually make while navigating traffic in such a situation, and called home, where my husband was watching the weather guys on television and doing his best to stay calm. He confirmed the weather was nasty, said "heavy rotation" had been spotted in the area, and asked if I had anywhere to go. I didn't.

We hung up. I turned off the radio because it wasn't doing anything but making my blood pressure rise, and put every ounce of concentration and attention into getting myself home.

And then came a mighty gust of wind came so quick and powerful that I had no time to even respond to it, and off the highway came my car in a fast spin across the pavement..

I braced my entire body, forced my eyes to stay open, locked my hands on the wheels and prayed "OhGodOhGodOhGod" with complete desperation until the car stopped. I remember my stomach reeling, my mind scrambling as I tried unsuccessfully to stay focused. To the best my recollection, I think I spun one full rotation and then skidded to a stop just inches from the guard wall and an exit ramp. I have no idea how or why I did not hit another car, ram into the concrete guard wall or fly into a nearby overpass.

Once I realized I was no longer moving, I remember taking a deep breath, checking to make sure I was out of the traffic lanes—and then bursting into tears. All around me the storm raged. And my car would not start up again. I did not know or care why. It was a terrifying few seconds. But after a moment, I also remember thinking, very clearly, and actually saying aloud, "I will not die today. Not like this." And then I looked out through the windows, all around me, trying to get some sense of what my options might be.

Just then, a car pulled off the road in front of me, coming to a stop just past where I'd landed, flashers on. In a split second, and with my car clearly not capable of taking me anywhere, I decided I needed company for whatever choice I was going to make. Throwing my black leather Sunday-best heels on the floor, and stashing my cell phone in my bra so it stood a chance of staying dry, I ducked out of my car, barefoot, slammed the door shut with my whole body against the still-raging wind and rain, and ran to the other car and pounded on its passenger window.

A young couple in their twenties, working their way home to Indiana from a vacation in Florida, urged me into their car, soaking wet mess though I was. They'd stopped, as it turned out, because they'd seen my car fly across the interstate and thought whoever was driving that flying car might need help.

We made it to the next exit, me and this couple (I never even knew their names). And at that exit we pulled off and into the shelter of some low buildings and thick tree cover. I think we probably made the sort of nervous conversation strangers sometimes do in situations in which they are thrown together, but I don't remember any of it. In a little while the storm began to die down, and the skies became somewhat visible. And my cell phone rang. On the other end were Michael and Lisa, friends who had also been at the ordination. They'd just driven past my car, realized I wasn't in it, and so were looking for me. With help from the young couple, I was able to give Michael directions to where we were, and he and

Lisa came and got me and took me to their home in Lexington and gave me dry clothes and a stiff drink and called my husband to say, "We've got her. She's safe."

It was a full year or so before I told my parents the true story of that day. How scary it had been. How lost I'd felt. How beyond grateful I was for the hospitality I was shown by strangers and friends alike. I remain grateful, because I suspect—at the edges of my conscience—that I was in much more immediate and grave danger than I ever really knew that day. And yet, somehow, a most unlikely series of events unfolded to shelter me.

⁂

Just over a year later, a storm that made my own experience seem child's play in comparison let loose its wrath along the coast of Louisiana, and the lives of millions of people were never the same. The city of New Orleans, in its entirety, has never been the same. I have never been to New Orleans, and so if I were to visit now, all I'd know is its status post-Katrina. I would feel sadness, I am sure, but I cannot truly understand just how it is for those who lived in and loved that city before.

A decade has passed since Hurricane Katrina. And the ugly truth is that parts of New Orleans still lie in ruins. And all over the United States, perhaps all over the world, are people who can witness to their entire life trajectory changing—relocation, job changes, financial ruin, lost family members—in the wake of Katrina's fury.

I was serving as the youth minister at Crestwood Christian Church in Lexington when Katrina came. And on September 1, 2005, I wrote these words:

> *I cannot believe that what I'm seeing on TV hour after hour is real—much less that it is happening just a day's drive from my front door. I'm almost ashamed at my own ethnocentricity— "Not here! Not in the United States!" I stumble over the word refugee—it feels uncomfortable and awkward when used to*

refer to Americans—and yet it's the only word that can even begin to capture the hell that these children of God are living.

I want to do something—to fill my basement with cots and hold the hands of frightened strangers while they sleep on those cots. I want to fill a car with warm food and needed medicine and clean water and take it to those who need those things. I feel so helpless, so unable to do anything in the wake of such devastation. I want to reach into my television and offer some sort of comfort. The insanity of it all is surreal, stories I would expect to hear from a war zone. Someone today described it as apocalyptic—and I cannot find a better word.

And in the midst of all this I am looked to as a leader, as someone who can help make sense of it all. On Sunday, I will be expected to speak of God's love. I'm not sure I can do it. I don't know how to celebrate creation right now. The people most directly affected must feel so betrayed by this very earth that sustains us. What do I say, what do I do in the face of it all? How can I offer hope to people who I know are going to be seeking it when I cannot see anything but more misery in the days ahead?

It is in times such as these that I need a living, flesh-and-bone God. My cry of anguish is only one in thousands—and if my own soul aches so tremendously, how much more must the souls of those who suffer directly be shattered and sore? In this is a vivid and cruel reminder that we are not invincible. Security and control are such grand illusions, carefully constructed walls meant to make us feel better about the unpredictable nature of this world we live in.

In all this, though, we must find a way to God. I do not know that way just yet—I am not sure I can speak with any authority of God's goodness. But what I keep coming back to, even in the fear and horror, is this simple truth—that we must believe God is with them, that God's heart is broken,

too, and that God's arms long to hold God's children in ways
we cannot fathom.

I must hold on with fierceness to faith that somewhere beyond
the flood waters and the vanished homes and the death and
destruction and violence is God, calling us to please help, to
please live compassion, to please build hope out of what has
been lost.

The next afternoon, the staff at Crestwood received word hundreds of Katrina refugees might be coming to Lexington. In the storm's aftermath there was a mad rush to get people somewhere, anywhere, safe. Lexington was one of many cities in the Southeast "on hold" to receive Katrina refugees.

We, of course, offered Crestwood as a shelter location, specifically our large Mission Center: a full kitchen, gym, flex space, and multiple classrooms of varying sizes. The next day a Red Cross worker surveyed our facilities, asked a few questions about volunteer power and resources, and then immediately approved us as an emergency shelter. She was efficient. Authoritative. A little gruff and strict in her approach, but also obviously grateful for our willingness to offer shelter. Prepare for 200–300 visitors, we were told—men, women and children.

How does one prepare for such a thing? We weren't sure, but we did our best. A few days later, with the guidance of the Red Cross and well over 100 church volunteers, we set about the task of turning Crestwood inside out. Every activity scheduled in our Mission Center moved to a different part of the church building or to another location off-site entirely. Sunday school classes and youth group activities and meetings all shifted. Our kitchen was cleaned out, our classroom space cleared to make room for the donations of blankets and bottled water and diapers and toothbrushes that poured in. A shower schedule was arranged (how do over 200 strangers share four showers?), a dining room set up, entertainment planned, food provided, hygiene concerns

thought out, security arranged, and shelter volunteers coordinated. In the course of one day, Crestwood Christian Church moved into half the amount of space we'd been using and our Mission Center was transformed into a miniature city. It was one of the brightest and most hopeful things I ever saw in over fifteen years of congregational ministry.

Close to 200 air mattresses, lovingly made up with sheets and blankets and brand-new pillows, covered the gym floor, with walking aisles the only floor space left. Those mattresses were inflated by grandmothers and grade school children and fathers—this amazing ant farm of all ages working together to create a welcoming space. I remember in particular little Judy, who couldn't have been more than five or six, grabbing my elbow and begging, as I sat huffing and puffing over a manual air pump, on my fifth mattress, "Miss Julie? Please, can I help? Please, can I do it?"

Of course she could. And she did. Working as hard as those of us five and ten times her age. It was a fine moment in time for all of us—elders and deacons and Sunday school teachers and new members and charter members and staff and volunteers all working together, never mind that some of us often didn't get along. Disputes over budgets or property or program faded and all that mattered was getting our church home ready for people who had lost their own homes. Their own everything.

However, the people never came. We stood ready, but they never came. The Bluegrass is a long drive from the Big Easy, and other, closer shelters were found. But in the preparing, and the waiting, and the wondering if and when they would come, and what it would be like when they did, I was reminded of "Would You Harbor Me?" a song sung by Sweet Honey in the Rock—the lyrics begin with, "Would you harbor a Christian, a Muslim, a Jew?" and they go on to name all the disenfranchised of this world, all those who inhabit the dark borders of our communities, the whispered edges of our neighborhoods and cities.

Who would we harbor? Who do we shelter? Who do we leave on their own, to survive whatever storm is raging in their lives or their hearts with whatever desperate measures they can muster?

Harbor and refuge are holy words for me, and so in the days following Katrina, even when a well-meaning church member challenged me, angrily, on my use of the word *refugee* to describe those left with nothing in the storm's wake, I insisted upon the word I'd chosen to use. "God is my refuge," the psalmist wrote—making us all refugees who seek the safe harbor of God's agape love. I spoke refuge with reverence, knowing that the word represented men and women and children whose lives had been changed in ways most horrific.

I used it to describe people who needed a great and mighty rock to cling to—as we all, to varying degrees, sometimes do; as our children, even in their beautiful and innocent resilience, often do. There is so much in this world that threatens their safe growth and development.

Threats like heroin, once again an epidemic in our country.

Threats like human trafficking, a booming business that operates nowhere near as far away from our schools and neighborhoods and churches as we'd like to believe it might.

Threats like the accessibility of guns designed solely for the purpose of killing other human beings (and even target-marketed to little girls via pink stocks).

Threats like cyber-bullying—so prevalent, and so easy to hide.

Threats like young black men having to take seriously their physical safety every time they so much as walk to the corner store, such a bias exists against them in our nation.

Threats like the suicide and depression and homelessness rates of LGBT youth—and so many more that listing them would leave

any of us believing there was no point in hoping, not when our world is so violent, so brutal, so unforgiving.

It is, for us and our children, a stormy world. And, so, how do we offer our children shelter in the midst of such constant and brutal buffeting, even as we often experience the buffeting ourselves? And how do we do so while keeping in sight and mind the goodness also present in the world?

I have no definitive answers for this, but I suspect that it lies in offering them shelter from the storms. And this means our children must have places and people in their lives that help them feel safe. Protected. Given refuge.

Louisville, Kentucky, is home to National Safe Place, a nonprofit begun in 1983 with the intent of making sure troubled or in-trouble youth have a safe place to go when such a place is needed. Safe Place incorporates a vast network of volunteers and designated safe locations across the country, so that if a teenager suddenly finds he or she has nowhere to go and be assured of safety, he or she can look for one of the telltale yellow "Safe Place" signs at a gas station or a library or a McDonald's—or any number of common buildings or businesses—and someone in that place will know where the teenager can go and how he or she can get there. Immediate shelter in a storm.

Don't we all need such immediate shelter—albeit even if figuratively—at some point in our lives?

Writer Anne Lamott often quotes lifelong spiritual seeker Ram Dass as saying, "We're all just walking each other home." And if this is true—and I certainly believe it is—then our greatest shelter is found in one another, in remembering we do not journey alone. And so, when storms do come—and they will, in all shapes and sizes and from all kinds of sources and situations and from all directions—perhaps our greatest strength is found in simply reaching out for the closest and most willing hand and asking, "Can I just hold this for a while?"

When Maddy was very small and she wanted to be picked up, held, she'd raise her little arms high in the air and say to Mommy or Daddy or any nearby known adult, "Hold you?" Not, "Hold me," or "Pick up?" or anything like that...no, "Hold you?" And of course we always did.

I wonder, now, if maybe that is the perfect thing to say. Because really what she was asking was to hang on to us for a while, to be kept up close and safe for a bit.

Fred Rogers, known to millions of us as "Mr. Rogers," died in 2003. His legacy lives on in countless ways, perhaps most of all in a story he told in a variety of places—that, when he was young, and afraid because of some world event he was seeing on the news, his mother would tell him, "Look for the helpers," and assure him that he'd always see people helping those in need. Thankfully, I have known this to be true in my own observations and experiences. Even in the mighty and terrible face of September 11, 2001, there were helpers to be found—men and women who risked their lives to help, assist, and shelter those who needed it.

Look for the helpers in any storm, and you'll see people who have found a way to maintain calm and nonanxious presence in the midst of chaos. You'll see people working to create safe space. You'll see people working to remind those who are hurting or suffering the most, "You are not alone." You'll see people who, when someone asks, out of fear or desperation or both, "Hold you?" say, "Yes. Absolutely I will. Until you feel safe again."

And so maybe the best promise we can make our children is a promise to be their constant helpers through this life, assuring them that, in any storm, they will not be alone, and that we are there, always, to hold them fast and secure until a sense of safety has been restored.

≈ ≈

I'm not sure how old she was when this happened. Old enough to talk in clear and complete sentences. Young enough to still need a full car seat, not a booster. We were leaving my office after a church board meeting that had run late, and I was anxious to get home for two reasons. One, I was worn out from a long day. Two, there was volatile weather brewing, and during the board meeting, multiple folks had been keeping an eye on the weather via phone and laptop.

Before we made it out of the church parking lot, the predicted storms broke loose. With sound and fury.

"It's raining, Mommy!" Maddy hollered from the backseat. "It's a storm!"

"I know baby," I said. "It's okay."

I believed my own words right up until I realized roads were washing out entirely too quickly, the ground still saturated from fierce rains earlier in the week. Already water was rising and it was slow and treacherous going. Lightning bolted, thunder roared, wind blew, and I fought to maintain control over my knee-jerk reaction to driving in such weather (panic, and perhaps rightfully so, given other such stormy driving experiences).

And then I heard my sweet girl's voice. At the top of her preschool lungs she was singing a medley of, "Rain, rain, go away! Come again another day!" and, "It's raining, it's pouring, the old man is snoring!" Thankful that she'd found a way to actually enjoy the moment, I focused on getting us home safely, navigating through two stalled cars, three flooded intersections, and wind blowing hard enough to send water crashing down on my windshield every few moments. Finally, we turned onto the street that would lead us directly to ours, and, as we did, Maddy's tune changed. I laughed out loud, stormy weather and all, when I heard her sweet high voice singing, "Jesus' love is bubbling over, Jesus' love is bubbling over, Jesus' love is bubbling over, AL-LE-LU-IA!"

She didn't stop belting out songs until we pulled up against the sidewalk in front of our house, and, once inside, began chattering happily to Daddy about everything from the rain to her most recent and imagined "boo-boo." I headed straight for the kitchen, poured a glass of wine, and sat down, glad to feel the tension in my neck slowly releasing and my heart rate beginning to feel normal.

Maybe she realized I was too quiet, or maybe she just knows when something is bothering someone she loves—either way, I was all at once humbled and filled with gratitude when she broke away from her dad long enough to look me in the eye and say, "Mommy? Did the rain scare you?"

"Oh, Maddy," I said, fighting back the tears I could feel building up against my eyelids, "Mommy *was* scared. But you know what? Your singing helped me an awful lot."

"Oh," she said, clearly not really understanding what I had told her, but somehow, I think, grasping that everything was all right. With a smile and a skip and a new song escaping her tiny pink lips, she ran off to play, and I prayed that she'd always feel so safe and so loved.

I prayed she'd always find shelter when storms come.

Chapter 7

ADAM

O n our drive to school one morning, Maddy asked, "Mommy, what if we lived in a world with third chances?"

Her question struck me as both odd and thought-out, and so I answered, "Can you tell me what you mean by that?"

"What if we had third chances, not just second ones?" she said, and then added, "because, you know, if we had third chances, Adam might not be in jail."

Ah. Adam. And then I remembered she'd seen me reading a letter from him the week before, and, as always, had asked, "When will I meet Adam, Mommy?"

And I'd answered, as always, "I don't know. But I hope soon."

At fifteen years old, my world didn't extend much beyond the triangle created by (1) the house I lived in, (2) the high school I went to, and (3) the church where my dad served as pastor. These three physical landmarks were all within a square mile of each other.

Kids from all walks of life traversed the halls of Winder-Barrow High School. That said, they did so in a pretty well-defined socioeconomic, cultural, and ethnic order. The hallways of my high

school were segregated much like the town itself. Exceptions were our starting running back, a few star basketball players, a couple of really talented young black musicians, and one or two black kids from very wealthy families.

I was completely absorbed in this world, unable to see much past whatever was happening in it on any given day, when Adam showed up in my life.

Easter - 1991

Our family with Adam

Home after school one afternoon, curled up on the den couch with my nose jammed in that week's reading assignment for English literature, I heard Dad's truck pull up in the driveway. I unwound long legs and scrambled up to open the door for him, dropping my teenage jaw in wonder and disbelief as Dad walked around from behind his car door carrying a scared little boy with liquid brown eyes peering out from beneath curly dark hair. "This is Adam," Dad said. "He's going to stay with us for a while."

The rest of the story came out in bits and pieces over the course of the afternoon, as my mom, sister, and I scrambled to make room for Adam. Dad was the minister "on-call" for the local

benevolent association that month, and on the day Adam arrived, he'd somehow fielded a call about a woman named Linda who was being admitted into a psychiatric hospital unit. Linda was single and broke and didn't have any family around. She lived in a tiny rundown house in a part of town where no one lived by choice. She was also the mother to a preschooler named Adam, any father figure long gone. Linda was unable to provide much more than a roof over his head. Adam had, quite literally, nowhere else to go without his mom around, and that night he slept on a makeshift pallet next to my parents' big bed.

If confession truly is good for the soul, then my own soul has been treated well, for I have confessed multiple times that Adam's abrupt arrival in our lives caused me no end of selfish adolescent embarrassment. I was petrified of what my friends would think of this random child tagging along with the Richardsons, his coffee-with-cream-colored skin a dead giveaway that, while Linda may have been white, Adam's father surely wasn't. While this would have been notable in many places, in the small Southern town I grew up in, it was much more than just noticed.

Adam's arrival also meant my sister and I had to rearrange our afternoon schedules to babysit him. Mostly, Adam felt like a major interruption of my sophomore year, and I was none too happy about it.

It's easy to assume and judge. And I did then. But I know now that Linda fell into that category of the alone and untreated mentally ill whose lives are scraped out in whatever way possible, sometimes at the expense of others. Truthfully, Linda did the best she could with what she felt was available to her, having long ago learned to work to her advantage a system she had no hope of escaping.

A week or so after Adam's arrival, I found myself home alone with him. I still didn't really know exactly how to interact with this kid. He didn't talk much, and mostly I just let him do his thing. That afternoon, though, he walked quietly up to me, and held up

a book—one he'd just chosen from the pile of children's books Mom had dragged out of the basement his first night with us. I took the book from his little hands, pulled him up with me on the same couch I'd been curled up comfortably on the day he arrived, and began to read.

Before I could protest or prevent it, Adam had curled himself into my lap, his head nestled under my chin and his thumb stuck firmly in his mouth, and this is how we remained until Dad showed up with the abrupt news that Adam was leaving.

With the feigned nonchalance only a teenager can pull off, I handed Adam over to Dad, even opening the front door to help them out. And, then, as Dad put Adam in the car, no words about whether or not we'd ever see him again, and nothing much else except, "His mom's come home, Julie," from my dad, I closed the door and collapsed against it in tears, so in love with Adam and so ashamed of my initial reaction to him.

For the next decade or so, Adam drifted in and out of our lives. Local social workers and school counselors learned to call Mom and Dad when there was a problem with homework or Adam needed money for lunch or a field trip. Linda went in and out of numerous treatment facilities. Sometimes Adam stayed with us for weeks, sometimes just a night. Upon arrival, he always smelled heavily of cigarette smoke, and oftentimes needed a bath. Those two issues were always quickly remedied, with Mom setting about the task of getting him fed, cleaned, clothed, and then immediately to the dining room table to do his homework. "Julie and Joy have to do their homework, too," she'd tell him, never giving in to the pleading of those deep brown eyes, holding steady over his protests.

Maddy says to me, of her grandmother, "Neana's strict!" I always laugh and say, "Tell me about it!" And Mom was—firm and insistent in her expectations of her children, and unfailing in her love for them, all three—the two she'd born, and the surrogate one she fell in love with along the way.

When Adam was in middle school, life happened—in other words, my sister and I had both moved away from home and married. My parents moved from Georgia to eastern North Carolina. And though I'm certain they'd have taken Adam along without a moment's hesitation, he was, after all, not truly (read: *legally*) ours. Adam had a mother. And, in her own way, and as much as she could, she loved him.

College. Graduate school. New families created and new babies born. New jobs across the board for all of us along the way, and, in the midst of all of it, we lost track of him.

And then we found him. We'd been doing Internet searches for a while, with no luck. But arrest records aren't private—and so when Adam's name popped as an accomplice to the armed robbery of a fast-food joint not far from where Adam and I had grown up, we were able to access his photo and his location in the state prison system.

I've seen scary mug shots, the sorts of things that get posted on the nightly news or printed in the local paper. But all I could see in Adam's arrest photo was the now-grown face of the little boy I loved, albeit the years of trouble showing in his countenance.

A dear friend of mine serves as a chaplain at a state prison in Kentucky. The inmates he works with have been convicted of some of the most horrible things you can imagine—things you don't even want to imagine. "How do you stand it?" I've asked him. And he tells me what I know is true, even if I can't quite stomach it, "They are God's, too, Julie."

I've known people who have loved folks in prison. And, while I certainly admired their efforts, I never entirely understood the love and care a person could still feel for someone who'd done the world such intentional harm. I get it now; because, when I learned that Adam was an inmate at a state prison down South, my first, overwhelming thought was not, "What's he done?" It was, "Thank

God he's alive!" And I meant it. In those first few moments of knowing he was still out there, somewhere, my heart sang that we could still find a way to get to him.

Adam and I exchange letters now on a fairly regular basis. He calls Mom when allowed, and they correspond via mail as well. Mom and Dad both have visited him. Ordinary things make me think of him. Harry Potter. He inhaled the first of the Potter series when it came out. I began the series shortly thereafter in an effort to answer my parents': "I wonder why he loves that book so much?" Or Pokemon, his end-all obsession at age ten. Or the movie *Aladdin,* which I once watched with him. "I still know the words to the songs from that movie, Julie," he once wrote to me, "and sometimes I sing them to cheer myself up." I took him ice-skating once, too, and I can't go to an ice rink without laughing at the memory of his spindly ten-year-old legs careening madly across the smooth surface and smashing into the sides of the rink, much to the amusement of my then-boyfriend and me.

There is no way of knowing for sure what will happen to Adam. This is true for anyone, but in his case it begs questions like Maddy's: "When do I get to meet Adam, Mommy?"

Adam's story—my story of life connected to him—only matters to any wider audience because it is the truest personal example I know of having been transformed by relationship. The possibility relationships have of transforming our lives and hearts is, I believe, our surest and most tangible expression of hope. And the modeling of transformational relationships is, I think, one of the greatest gifts we can offer our children.

If you want to take a Christian view of it, it is the heart of the gospel. God loved God's people and creation so much, and was so heartbroken over the ways those people and creation were failing to be what they were created to be, that God decided it was time to come among the people. Among creation. In an actual flesh-and-blood person who could be touched, held, loved, cast aside,

scorned. A person who could burrow deep under our skin and make us question everything we thought we knew about the world and our place in it. A person who could challenge us, critique us, call us to something better in our ways of being. A person who reached out to those on the very fringes of society—those misunderstood, feared, and judged and said, "You. I want *you* to be my friend."

When I was doing youth ministry, I once worked with a young man who had Asperger's Syndrome. Andrew was often hilarious and clearly brilliant. He was also, as is typical of people with Asperger's, socially unaware and difficult to understand. Being his friend was a challenge to the others in the youth group, though most of them rose to it graciously.

One summer, I took Andrew and about twenty other teenagers on an international mission trip. Think mostly white, relatively affluent, tech-savvy, suburban teenagers dropped unceremoniously into the landscape of a poverty-stricken Caribbean island nation. It was a long, hot, frustrating week, and not one of us, youth or adults, were anywhere near a comfort zone.

About midweek, just when the pressure cooker of life together had reached maximum containment, Andrew was assigned to paint the exterior cement block wall of the mission site bathhouse with two of his youth group peers. One was Josh, who was popular and funny—a good kid who excelled at sports and was otherwise just so kind and decent that being his friend was easy for most folks. Josh had known Andrew since they were in the church nursery together, and while they didn't always get along, they at least knew how to deal with one another.

Tony, however, was pretty new to the whole youth group scene, and he was, to put it kindly, a work in progress in terms of his ability to be part of the group. He was often combative if crossed, and played at the edges of bullying in a way that was hard to catch or define. He could just as easily charm as harm anyone he chose.

It wasn't long before Tony and Andrew locked horns. And Tony, being the more socially adept of the two, and having found more than a few chinks in Andrew's armor, amused himself by goading Andrew's frustration. At least, that's how Josh explained it to me later. I walked around the corner of that bathhouse, having heard heated voices, to find Andrew moments away from slinging a paint-laden roller brush at Tony's head, both of them with faces flushed, chests puffed out, and voices strained with frustration. Near them stood Josh, doing his best to diffuse the situation.

"Stop it!" Josh yelled to Tony and Andrew. And then, while I was still figuring out how to break up the impending physical altercation, Josh rose up in one quick move from where he was squatting to paint the bottom edge of the wall, lunged at Tony and locked his arms from behind. No one got to Andrew in time, and the roller brush went soaring, landing squarely on Tony's chest. Andrew stomped off. Josh stepped back from Tony. And Tony commenced to demand of me what I was going to do about "Andrew being an ass."

Before I could answer, out came Josh's angry words, "No, Tony. You can't treat Andrew that way. You just can't talk to him that way and expect him to deal with it. You know better. From now on, you leave him alone!"

Josh stalked off in search of Andrew, and Tony never bothered Andrew again.

Andrew and Josh—they had a relationship—one born of having known each other their whole young lives. And if Andrew's way of being in the world was sometimes too much for most folks, Josh didn't see it that way. Andrew was Andrew. And Andrew was ours. He was part of us. And so we would love him and protect him as best we could, even when it wasn't pleasant or easy to do so.

Andrew and Josh lent me a little hope that day—hope for a kinder, gentler world for my daughter, and theirs.

In some ways, Josh's protection of Andrew that day reminds me of the gospel story of Jesus' protection of Zacchaeus. Zacchaeus was a tax collector—not exactly on everyone's "top five people I want to have over for dinner" list. Jesus didn't argue the point, he just made it clear that Zacchaeus was part of the community too, so much so that Jesus was going to sit down at Zacchaeus' kitchen table and share a meal and conversation together. No big lecture to those who thought he was crazy for doing so. No specific sermon on why he was reaching out to Zacchaeus and what the ramifications of it might be. No. He just did it. He just entered into relationship with someone on the fringe, and, in doing so, made it clear that we are called to do likewise.

Offering up Andrew's story as one of hope means also acknowledging the other side of things. If I had any part in helping Andrew navigate his teenage years by being in relationship with him, I failed at doing the same with Tony. He wandered in and out of youth group for a year or so, finally drifting off permanently. I saw him a few months after his last appearance at church quite by accident—in a city park, his back turned to me like the three other young men he stood with, all of them clutching surreptitiously at brown paper bags, with the faint smell of pot rolling off their bodies. I remember thinking it was best to walk quietly and quickly past, and I did, but not without a tinge of deep sadness at it all.

Because, Jesus might have invited himself to dinner at Tony's place, too.

And so it goes that all relationships are difficult things, complex by their very nature, and some of them bring out what's worst in us, while others help us thrive and become more of who we're meant to be.

And some of them change us entirely—transforming us into something we never knew we could be. Sometimes we're lucky, and they make us better people than we ever knew we could be.

Adam once wrote to me from his prison cell, "I love that you and your sister [a social worker] do things that make a difference in the world. Maybe I helped that because maybe I was the first person you made a difference in the life of."

It was quite a while before I could read the rest of the letter after that, his words having brought a rush of tears. You see, I understand it very differently.

What I see, what I understand, is that it was Adam who made the difference—the one who burrowed under the self-conscious skin of a teenage girl and helped her see how beautiful though broken the world can be. It's Adam, who will for the rest of his life walk around with the label "convict," who taught me what it means to love without label and who gave me a deeper understanding of what it means to be in relationship with someone despite everything that would point you to the contrary.

If the world handed me beauty through no earning it of my own, it also handed Adam brokenness through no fault of his own. And because of what we were each handed, our lives unfolded in very different ways. And yet, in my life—and in his—dwells beauty and brokenness both. And, somewhere between, hope dwells. For both of us.

And, I think, somehow, too, for little girls who believe in third chances. Maddy firmly believes that Adam deserves another chance. And perhaps she's on to something. Perhaps she knows something about God's unconditional and redemptive love for God's children that we adults often forget. Perhaps she knows, deep in her precious bones, that God has not left Adam. And because of this, she knows that God will never leave her, either.

Chapter 8

GRANDDADDY

"Hey, Cuz!" Noah called from the corner of the attic where he half-stood, half-knelt, straddling a gap in the attic floor to reach the object of his desire. I smiled when I saw my cousin's fist holding up an old green knapsack—Army issue. "I knew it! A military man never gets rid of his stuff!"

Until the day before, Noah and I had only seen each other once in fifteen years. Raised on separate coasts and the children of a brother (his dad) and sister (my mom) who weren't all that great about keeping in touch despite their love for one another, he and I might as well have been strangers. Except that morning we'd sat side by side in a tight funeral home pew, my shoulders rounded in a grief I didn't quite understand, his shoulders ramrod straight in his Marine dress blues.

And now this afternoon we found ourselves together—laughing and telling stories and searching through piles of dust-coated clutter in an attic neither of us had been in since we were very small in hopes of finding out something about our grandfather, John Louis Jones.

He'd died. And we'd come to say goodbye.

≈ ≈

There's an old picture, circa 1979, of me standing next to Granddaddy at what I've been told is a clay pigeon shoot. No

one believes me when I say that I remember that day; I'm wearing a jacket in the picture, but it's sunny, and I remember being warm. I tagged along after Granddaddy while he traded stories and jokes with friends and acquaintances, stopping at some point to buy me a Mello Yello. My parents and toddler-aged sister were close by, though I've no idea where. My daughter's round rosy cheeks are a gift from me, and that's evident in my face in this picture.

Granddaddy and me at a clay pigeon shoot circa 1979

The truth is that such vivid memories of him are hard to come by. Most are clouded by the fifteen years he was absent from my life. When I was just beginning middle school, he and my grandmother divorced after roughly forty years of marriage. Rightly or wrongly, Granddaddy received the greatest amount of blame for this; and, as is often the case in such situations, there was too much hurt for any of us to successfully work our way through, and physical distance made it easy to let it all go.

I hadn't seen him in close to fifteen years, but I recognized the bald head shining dimly through the restaurant's windows. "That's him, guys," I said, "He's here already," and at my words a familiar tension settled into the minivan containing my mother, my mom's younger sister (my Aunt Lela), her family, and me. My three cousins, much younger than me and knowing nothing about

our shared grandfather's estrangement from his family, all began exclaiming excitedly, and I found myself breathing a sigh of relief at their presence, hopeful it might provide distraction during what had all the warning signs of being a difficult evening.

It was just after Christmas, and Grandma had just died. We'd all—my mom, Aunt Lela, my uncles (Ted and John), and all the respective families— converged on the tiny town of Selmer, Tennessee, an hour east of Memphis. It seemed awkward, at best, to not make an attempt at seeing their father, their mother's ex-husband, especially when he'd made an effort to come to Grandma's visitation and his grandchildren were all in town for the first time in who knows when—certainly not since he and Grandma had divorced.

And so there we were, crowded around an old wooden table at Pusser's Restaurant, notable for its deep-fried onion rings and for having been named after Selmer's great claim to fame, Buford T. Pusser, the fabled sheriff who'd once waged war against moonshiners and the like, portrayed by Joe Don Baker in *Walking Tall* back in 1973. We got through dinner that night with everyone being politely kind to one another. My younger cousins entertained us. Mom and Aunt Lela did their best to talk to their dad, their deep grief for their mom, I'm sure, making that even more difficult. I did my best to be present, to engage in it all as best I could. My own sister was not with us. Joy was in India, on a three-week study trip for graduate school, and I was missing her presence very much.

Somewhere close to dessert, entirely against my stubborn will and for reasons I cannot explain, I felt the tight and cold place inside me, born of conflict and angst and years of no communication between my grandfather and me, begin to soften. The octogenarian I sat across from was old and tired and carried the weight of decades of difficulty in his worn face. That much was evident. Also evident was his deep, if very contained, gladness at being at the table at all. Despite the strained relationships, he seemed thankful to see

us—happy, even, that we'd come. Having recognized his gratitude, I couldn't help but want to respond to it.

And so, when the last bit of chocolate meringue pie had been eaten and we all stood to go, and Granddaddy insisted on the check, taking it quietly to the cash register, I followed him. As we stood waiting for him to finish paying, the cashier asked, "These folks all your family, Mr. Jones?" Before he could say a word, and almost without thinking, I offered up, "I'm his oldest granddaughter." And as the words left my mouth, I felt Granddaddy's arm curl around my waist for the first time since I was in grade school, and a shy smile broke across his face.

I smiled, too, and that was the beginning of the brokenness being named and healed.

Make no mistake, it wasn't all reconciliation and roses after that. When a relationship has stagnated and been broken, no matter the reason, it is very difficult to begin a path to something that resembles wholeness. For the next couple of years I still didn't see or hear from Granddaddy much, though I often asked my mom about him, and she seemed to be more in touch with him than she'd been throughout my adolescence.

Along the way, Maddy was born, and when she was just north of two, Granddaddy's health took a sharp decline. When that happened, I realized something I wish desperately I'd realized sooner—my grandfather was my daughter's only living great-grandparent. The only one of my grandparents who'd ever actually been alive at the same time as her.

This, perhaps more than anything, prompted me to pick up the phone and call him. My fingers trembling as I dialed, my insides mush as I managed, "Hi Granddaddy; it's Julie," and my heart bursting as he replied, "Julie! Well, how are you, honey?"

I assured him I was fine and asked how he was. I told him I was just calling to say "Happy Memorial Day," the only reason I could

think of to call and a valid one given that he was a World War II veteran. I made a hasty exit from the phone call, not at all sure what to talk to him about, but not before we were both able to get out, "I love you." I hung up the phone and cried. Maddy asked, as only an inquisitive and sensitive toddler can, "Mommy, why cry?"

"Because I just did something very important, baby," I said as I pulled her close, adding, silently, in the privacy of my own heart, "and because when I told Granddaddy I loved him, much to my own surprise, I meant it."

Barely six months later, Dad called one cool fall morning, "Julie, I just wanted to tell you your grandfather has died." I was sitting at my desk at work, prepping for a busy holiday season in youth ministry, and I remember quietly ending the phone call, putting my forehead to my desk, and letting the tears for my grandfather fall.

I'd called him a week before, my first call since that Memorial Day. He'd told me, "Oh, I'm fine, don't you worry!" when we both knew he wasn't and, again, I told him I loved him. And, again, I'd meant it.

❧ ❧

During my childhood and adolescence, I never knew much about my grandfather's military service, only the glossed-over stories he'd told when I was very young, stories about toughing it out in a prison camp. I'd no idea really, until much later, what prison camps even were, and so I just had these vague notions of my grandfather as some kind of semi-hero of a war I knew little about. Even as I grew older, learned more about our nation's history, saw *Saving Private Ryan*, read Tom Brokaw's *The Greatest Generation*, and heard stories from church members of that generation who were decorated war veterans, I still, somehow, never really connected all that to my own grandfather's service. In retrospect, this makes no sense to me. How could I have kept him so disconnected in my thoughts and learnings?

When *Unbroken* came out, the story of Louis Zamperini by Laura Hillenbrand, after I'd inhaled every word of it, most often through tears, I wanted to know more—suspecting, accurately, that Granddaddy's shiny war tales were mostly half-truths meant to satiate the curious questions of a little girl.

The whole truth is much more devastating. Our family has, through various World War II historical resources, pieced together bits of Granddaddy's story, and what we know for sure is this:

On July 19, 1944, Silver Slipper, the first nonpainted B-17 to fly in combat with the 8th Air Force, took off for a mission over central Germany. Silver Slipper's crew included Radio Technical Sergeant John L. Jones. Shortly after dropping its load of bombs, the plane was heavily damaged by anti-aircraft guns. For forty-five minutes they limped west, hoping to make France or England, but the engines overheated and the crew had to bail out.[1]

Despite their efforts to evade the Nazis, Granddaddy, and I assume several other of his unit, were captured and subsequently imprisoned in a camp. And in the last months of the war, in the bitterness of a cold German winter, he was marched across the countryside, as so many men were, many of them to their deaths.

I have no idea if my grandfather's prison camp experience was truly anything like Louis Zamperini's. But I know it must have been hell. And when I learned that my grandfather had spent the entire last year of the war in such a camp, my heart broke.

His much-younger brother, my mom's Uncle Jimmy, the only one of Granddaddy's many siblings left alive, says that he remembers his big brother coming back from war frightfully skinny—and also silent, the stories of what he'd endured locked inside him.

We understand the private pain of veterans so much better now, and still, we're just scraping the surface of what it is like for them

---

[1] I am grateful to the American Air Museum in Britain's website for some of the detail here. What we know we did not hear from the man who lived it.

to witness such horror, or, worse yet, be subjected to that horror, and then try to assimilate to life back home. I make no excuses for the years of no communication between my grandfather and me. I wish I'd known to reach out, had some sense that something else besides brokenness was possible.

And I cannot speak for his children. My mother and her siblings span sixteen years between the four of them—my mother the oldest and her sister the youngest. The household my mother came of age in was much different than the one my aunt did. I know very little of my uncles' thoughts on their lives as the sons of John Louis Jones. Ask each of the four children his or her perceptions of what their childhood was like, and I am confident you'd get four different answers. I know this much to be true—they grew up in a household in which there was a great deal of pain and heartache and a profound lack of communication. I also know that today they are all successful, caring adults with beautiful families and an abiding love for one another. This tells me that something, somewhere, went right—even if, perhaps, it was just the merciful work of grace winding itself through a fractured family, such that not all was lost.

What learning to love my grandfather again taught me is there is so much I do not know. So much I'll never understand. Relationships shatter on the floors of the houses they are built in all the time, and rarely are we able to fully grasp why. Granddaddy was a broken man, to be sure, and I imagine often an unpleasant and angry man in his brokenness. Maybe this was all a response to whatever he experienced in Germany. Maybe not.

∽ ∼

When I was very small, and we'd visit Grandma and Granddaddy, I would creep out of the house with him just before dawn, follow him across the pasture of their farm—frost crunching under our shoes—and stand beside him, trying to help, while he filled big wooden troughs with cow feed. And, half scared and half excited,

I'd do everything in my power to stay put while he called the cows from across the field and they'd come running for breakfast. Those large lumbering beasts galloping across that field petrified me, and it was all I could do not to run. But I didn't run. I knew I was safe. Granddaddy was next to me.

He has been gone for over five years now, and my thirst for knowledge about World War II has only increased during that time. So, too, has my capacity for forgiveness. Of myself. Of him. Of the myriad ways we all hurt the very ones God has called us to protect. So often, far too often, we are not our best selves.

My paternal grandfather died almost two decades before I was even born. My maternal grandfather—well, his story as I know it has been told here. Given these two realities, it is no surprise that one of my greatest joys is watching Maddy play with my own father. In their relationship is a healing of what has been, and a promise that something more is ahead.

We so often define people—those we know personally and those we know only from *People* or whatever news story is trending on Twitter—by their absolute worst moments, and in doing so make the sum total of their lives whatever their transgressions or sorrows have been, as opposed to seeing a person's whole life.

This is not how God defines us.

There is hope to be found in searching for what is good in a person. Remembering Granddaddy has taught me this. I know this is not always possible, and I ache with sorrow for those for whom abuse or violence or emotional trauma has meant the final dissolution of relationships. And I applaud those who know that for their own safety and well-being they must walk away from a friend or family member.

But thankfully, for me there is no longer a cold place in my heart when I think of my grandfather. Rather, I now find there a tender spot of mercy, of forgiveness, and gratitude that he is at peace from

all that raged inside him. And now, when I think of him, it is of the moments that mattered most—calling the cows for breakfast, tagging along after him across the garden, standing tall and proud to say to the waitress at Pusser's, "I'm his oldest granddaughter," and knowing, as I said it, that no person, no family, no life, is ever entirely perfect. But, in each of us dwells a bit of the God who created us, and so, always, there is hope that we can be what that same God has called us to be.

Chapter 9

BROKEN

One busy morning, when she was about three, Maddy was amusing herself by racing a large plastic car around the edges of the upstairs bathtub while I rushed to get ready for the day's work—I was serving a congregation as their youth minister then, and my day was stacked with meetings, program planning and production, and various visits with folks.

Maddy had already been bathed and dressed that morning, and until she started to play with the car, I'd forgotten to pull the drain plug, so the tub was still pretty full. As she *vroomed* the car around the tub edge, she'd dip the front end of the car into the water, enjoying the tiny splash it created. I was running late—this never brings out the best in me—and was preoccupied with sucking down what was left of my coffee, finding my keys, and slapping on mascara.

Suddenly, with a great flail of her arms and a squeal of glee, Maddy flung that plastic car with all her might into the still half-full bathtub. Water splashed all over the bathroom floor, dousing both my shoes and her outfit for the day. "Maddy! Stop it!" I yelled. "You're getting water everywhere!" She stopped. Put the toy car on the floor. And quietly went to her room. Without so much as a peep of protest or resentment. I sighed, blew out a heavy breath, and reached for the nearest bath towel to clean up.

And then, before I could even get bent over to sop up the wet, Maddy returned to the bathroom, just as quietly as she'd gone, dragging behind her purple pajamas with a pattern of hot pink hearts dashed across them, her head down and her shoulders slumped. "Mommy," she said, in a small voice, "I can clean up the water with these."

My heart crumbled into a sharp ache as she got down on her knees and began to mop up that water. With every ounce of humility I could muster, I got down on my knees next to her, pulled her into my lap and told her not to worry about that water. "I'm so sorry, kiddo. And I love you so much." And then together we cleaned up the bathroom.

In the grand scheme of things, it was not a big deal. I overreacted in a stressful moment, like every parent or caregiver does from time to time. But the memory stings, still, five years later. I regret it.

I don't often use the word *regret*—mostly because I believe our mistakes are often the things that hone us into the very human beings we are meant to be; and, too often, regret leads to the sort of guilt that eats at a person, holding her captive to her worst moments and defining her in terms of those moments.

And so, generally speaking, I find the word *sorrow* to be a more helpful one in thinking about the things in my life that I'd hoped would go differently, or that wouldn't happen at all. And one of my greatest sorrows is that my marriage dissolved somewhere around its fourteenth year. At the time, it felt like a line of dominos falling over faster than I knew how to handle, the conflicted pieces of our life together tumbling into one another and all of it crashing to the floor in anger and sadness and heartbreak.

In hindsight I understand it as more of a slow erosion, one in which I can certainly, now, with some distance, identify the crisis points over the years, and tell of the things that I wish I'd handled differently or that I wish hadn't happened at all.

My former husband is a good man—a fine pastor, and even finer father. It is important to me that this is said and that he and Maddy both know I believe it to be true. Clearly we had/have our share of differences, and I willingly admit having contributed my own deep flaws, mistakes, and fair share of pain to what became of us.

Often people ask, "What happened?" This is not particularly helpful. I recall one person even exclaiming, "Well, gosh, if two ministers cannot make a go of it, what hope do the rest of us have?" This was particularly painful. Maybe all the questions were well-intended. Maybe the askers of the questions were simply looking for some identifiable reason as to why two good people would end up divorced.

Still, it is no one's story but ours. And even I, having spent so much time and space in this very book telling stories, believe that some stories are best kept among those who painfully lived them.

Once, though, I was asked, "Do you regret marrying him?" To this I responded a quick and resounding, "No!" He made me a better person in many ways, even though I was not my best self at the end. And there were, of course, many beautiful days, some good memories for which I am still thankful. But most of all, my life with him gave us our daughter. She is, perhaps, the one thing we did best, and our great desire has been to continue to do right by her as her life has changed so dramatically, no matter the personal sacrifice this might require at times.

The hardest thing I've ever done in my life was tell her, "Daddy and I are getting a divorce." And yet even as I choked out the words in the calmest and, I hoped, most assuring voice I could, with her dad and I both there, each holding her little hands and all of us teary-eyed, I knew they were words that had to be said if the three of us were going to find any sort of way forward.

I'm profoundly grateful that, until that moment, Maddy had known, in her then seven years of life, only one house, with both

her parents in it, a village of family and friends who have loved her fiercely from the moment she showed up in the world, and a solid foundation of "I love you's," and "God loves you, no matter what." This has made all the difference in how she's been able to move forward.

My Grandma Jones grew daisies. Beautiful, bright, white daisies, with dark green leafy stems and tenacious roots. She was a genius at coaxing life from soil and tending to it once it had sprung. My grandmother has been gone for almost ten years, but her daisies live on—in Kentucky, in Tennessee, in North Carolina, and perhaps elsewhere, transplanted by my mother's capable hands and given to anyone who wanted some. That's how I know the roots of Grandma's daisies are so strong—they've survived change, propagated in the midst of new soil and new climate and even my own inexperienced hands. They are a living testament to my grandmother's own strength and resilience.

My daughter has this same strength. This same resilience. Maddy and Grandma's daisies have in common roots that have held them safe through transition. And, as Maddy, her dad, and I have learned a new normal, the roots have held, and new life has begun to prove its promise, even on days when I find myself wondering how I could have possibly gotten to this point, and wonder at my own worth, my own goodness, my own ability to both offer and seek forgiveness in the wake of it all.

Divorce comes with its own lion's share of stereotypes, its own allotment of gossip, and its own mythology about how it happens. And there are, of course, divorce horror stories—and far too many examples of adults using children as finely exacted weapons in their wars against one another.

However, I think mostly divorce happens in very ordinary ways to very good and ordinary people. This does not make it something to aspire to, by any means. Rather, it makes it all the more important that we talk about it, deal with it, offer real support to those going

through it. Scarlet letters, blame-casting, and finger-pointing do not, in the end, get anyone living through a divorce anywhere but deeper into his or her own personal hell.

What's needed most for families searching desperately for solid ground after having it crumble underneath them is space to grieve, hands to hold, and enough voices of mercy to combat the constant feelings of failure and heartache that journey with a person—be it an ex-husband, ex-wife, or a child finding herself with two homes—every day in the aftermath.

Just at summer's end before Maddy began third grade, she came down with a mild case of pneumonia. I'm a little paranoid about pneumonia, having once been leveled to five days in a hospital with an acute bacterial case of it, followed by a month-long recovery. Maddy bounced back relatively quickly, but still, her dad and I kept her home from her summer camp that week, instead taking her to work with each of us as the schedule dictated, and me mostly trying to work from home while she rested.

The last day of this arrangement, I had a 9:30 a.m. meeting at my office in Lexington—over an hour away from where we live in Louisville. That meant we had to get up, get ready, and get out by 8:00 a.m. to allow for any potential traffic snarls.

At 7:45, Maddy still wasn't dressed, despite my persistent prodding.

In retrospect, it was my fault. I shouldn't have let her watch an episode of *Good Luck Charlie* before insisting on clothes, teeth brushing, hair combing, etc. Still, she was plodding slow as proverbial molasses and I could feel the stress of being late for work rising in my chest. Truthfully, the entire situation had "plastic car in bathtub remix" written all over it—and I did not heed the warning signs very well at all.

"Maddy, come *on!*" I said, her insistent, "Hold on a minute!" only irritating me further. We went back and forth like this for several minutes, and finally, out the door we went, my displeasure obvious

in my tense and brisk walk to the car and the edge to my voice as I barked at her, "Get the lead out, Mads, c'mon!" as she trailed—deliberately, I'm sure—behind me.

She got in the car quietly, and as I jammed the key in the ignition, I caught a glimpse of her face in the rearview mirror. Her eyes were downcast and her mouth was downturned…just like the morning with the plastic car and the bathtub and the pajamas.

That's all it took for me to realize how ridiculous I'd been, acting like an insecure drill sergeant in my supposedly necessary haste to get out the door. The reality is my work folks wouldn't have begrudged me another fifteen minutes, and I knew this. I'd just chosen to ignore it in my desire for things to go my way, at my pace.

"Oh, honey," I said, reaching back to hold her hand in mine, "I am so, so sorry."

"It's okay," she said, not quite convincingly.

"No, no it isn't," I insisted. "I am worried about being on time for work and I had no right to talk to you that way. I'm really so sorry." And then I added, "Not even mamas are perfect."

"Mommy," she said, loud and clear and full of righteous truth, "no one is perfect."

I sat there. Quiet myself now. And I took a deep breath before saying, "Yes, I guess that's true. Where'd you learn that?"

"From you," she said, "I learned it from you." And I laughed. Out loud, with my head thrown back. First, because yes, she has learned it from me. Second, because, as she said those words with such full earnestness, all I could think of was the cheesy late 80s anti-drug commercial in which a father is screaming at his son, having found drug paraphernalia, and he demands, "Where did you learn this?" And son, sobbing and hysterical, screams back, "I learned it from watching *you*, okay?!? I learned it from watching *you!*"

The car ride to work went much better after my laughter and a round of heartfelt apologies.

Isn't this potentially true of so many conflicts?

I've struggled against the goal of perfection as long as I can remember, my own worst critic, slower to forgive myself for failings and mistakes than anyone else would ever be. I wanted to be the kid who always did it right, who was always approved of, who always excelled at everything she was good at. "I," as I once told a friend, "do not fuck up."

At least so I let the world believe. Let myself believe. To my own detriment.

I have intentionally covered up insecurity my whole life—if I thought myself fat, well, that was okay because I could sing. And I could write. And talent outweighed physical appearance, so never mind feeling uncomfortable in my own skin. If I thought myself not good enough at math, well, that was okay; no one expected someone like me who was good at speaking or reading or writing to also be good at math. So I never bothered to learn math and hid the pain of the tenth grade Algebra teacher's thoughtless remark, "You're just never going to get this, are you, Julie?" with my own professed hatred of numbers and formulas.

Denial and covering up only get you so far. Because, eventually life is about more than what you can do—it becomes about who you are. And it took me a very long time to figure that out how to be at home in the body and personality and way of being I'd been created with.

For Maddy, from the first moment I held her, I wanted her to know that perfection would never be required of her—that, if she didn't always make the best decisions, if she, too, struggled with infertility one day, if she wasn't the best in her class at everything... it would be okay; that all I ever wanted for her was for her to live into the beautiful potential she was born with as God's own child.

And so, over and over, even when I was having trouble remembering it myself, I'd tell her, "You don't have to be perfect."

Turns out she was listening.

If being a mother brought out more holy imperfection in me than I ever knew existed, becoming a divorcee sealed the sacred truth that I am indeed not perfect—that, like everyone else on this earth, I am capable of tremendous mistakes. I am capable of hurting another person out of my own pain and despair. I am full of as much darkness as I am light.

I use the words *holy* and *sacred* intentionally here, because the faith I profess is one full of stories of imperfect beings. While doing youth ministry I would tell this often to young people I worked with. I made sure they knew the stories of King David—liar, murderer, adulterer, and general vagabond. And yet he was God's chosen leader for God's chosen people of Israel. I told them about Peter—how he denied the very Jesus he'd sworn to follow in his worst and most fearful moment, but went on to spread Jesus' message of love and grace far and wide. I told them about Mary Magdalene—how no one else thought much of her and how she likely struggled with such demons, how she'd have been the girl at school everyone whispered about in the hallways. And yet Mary Magdalene was one of Jesus' closest friends and most faithful followers. I told them about Zacchaeus—a pathetic little man, indeed—and how Jesus stood by him anyway, and in a very public way, making it clear that Zacchaeus was worth Jesus' time and attention and care. Just as we all are.

I told these young people all these things, and begged them to see their worth as God's own. But, far too often, I failed to believe my own worth as God's own. This is true for so many of us. And I wonder how we're able to love anyone else at all when we so often are our own worst enemies.

Across the upper part of my right foot is a tiny, almost imperceptible scar. Across my lower abdomen is another scar, equally difficult to

see even though it is far more recent. A childhood game of hide and seek gotten out of hand gave me the one on my foot decades ago. Giving birth to Maddy gave me the second. One gash healed on its own—albeit raggedly. The other was stitched painstakingly together by the hands of a skilled surgeon. They are places my body was cut open by a foreign object, never to be quite the same again.

Once anything has been torn, broken, slashed, or ripped apart, it can never entirely be what it once was.

We all carry scars of one form or another—and, I suspect, if you were to crack open the chest of any one of us, gently pull back the sternum and peer into the soft folds and strong muscle of the heart, there'd be scars, there, too, marking the places where something's been broken. I have such a scar, I'm sure.

I once feared any such line being drawn across my heart, wanting no proof, no testament to any brokenness; now, I give thanks for it—because it is a scar born of facing imperfection and embracing grief long enough to allow them to condition me, strengthen me, grow me.

And so, once something has been broken, it can never be entirely what it once was. But it can be something different. Something stronger. Something more real. Sort of like that bunny in *The Velveteen Rabbit* that only became who he was meant to be after he'd just been worn and loved and played with to pieces. And, no matter the brokenness, the heart of us doesn't change. And God is present, perhaps most of all in the wild and unknown and still-full-of-grace patches in our lives. And, because of this, we get stitched together, even if with some tender spots along the ridges of the scarring.

It's true for all of us, this breaking apart and becoming whole again. It's part of life. And we don't get to escape it. There isn't anything special or unique about whatever has been broken in any of us. To think there is equals arrogance. And, so, maybe the most we can

hope for is that, having known brokenness, we'll be gentler with others, not so quick to judge, and much quicker to live the grace that has been so beautifully and abundantly woven through even the darkest moments of our lives.

An elderly woman in a congregation I once served handed me a tremendous gift one day. She emptied out her dining-room sideboard of the Fiesta plates and cups and platters and serving bowls held there and gave them to me. "I don't need them anymore," she said. "You take them. But bring me a picture of how pretty they all look set out on your dinner table." I collect Fiesta and she knew it, and I received her gift with a very grateful heart, and, even though I have newer, brighter pieces of Fiesta of my own, the ones she gave me are my favorites to use.

One piece in particular is a shade of teal that could have only been imagined circa 1970. Across it run several cracks, places where the plate broke and then was painstakingly glued back together by someone who shunned throwing anything away if it was at all possible to use it. "That one was mine," she said. "I used it so that company wouldn't have to, and that way guests never even knew it had been broken."

Most folks would have thrown it away, I suppose. I might have myself, except that in her telling me why she kept it, it became impossible for me to throw it out. I keep it in my kitchen cabinet, along with all the other Fiesta. I never use it, but I cannot bear to part with it.

That broken Fiesta plate helps me remember that life isn't perfect—that we are all, sooner or later, broken ourselves. Sometimes, this happens irreparably. But, more often than not, our brokenness is something to be valued, claimed as a the battle scar of life that it is and used to strengthen our resolve, firm our grip—even, perhaps, restore our hope.

My friend who gave me all that Fiesta knew something about brokenness. Her husband—the absolute center of her world—died

long before his time while she made an afternoon run to the grocery store. I heard her tell this story of finding his still and lifeless body, of dropping the groceries in horror, more times than I could count over the few years that I knew her, the pain of it still obvious in her every move and word. He'd left her alone—no children, and not much family to speak of. Though she never really talked about it, I suspect being childless wasn't a choice. It would have been rare for a couple of their generation to not have children. And I often wondered if, between her childlessness and the broken heart over her husband's death, there just remained too much sorrow for her to bear.

She died last year, and I wish I'd known more of her story. I wish she'd been willing to share more of her life with others; she was pretty closed off from the world by the time she died, having chosen to keep her hurts close to her heart, hidden from curious or wondering eyes. And she wore her grief as a mantle that was not to be disturbed.

Her brokenness, her heartache—it was hers alone.

Our children need us to do things differently. They need us to be honest about our fears and failings, open with our sadness and heartaches. Our children do not need to absorb them or carry them for us—no child should be drawn into parents' sufferings or conflicts or pain to the extent the child can no longer simply laugh and play and grow—but should be helped to realize, because we show them, that though we might experience things that bring us to our knees in fear or sorrow, we do not have to stay on our knees forever.

Our children need us to be real. To share our laughter. To show our fears. To rejoice together when there is something to celebrate. To cry together when the situation calls for it.

The stories of my own brokenness—they are not easy to share. Not at all. But I do it anyway, offering up out of my own experiences of

being broken, of bearing heartache, the ways that I have managed to move forward. I do it most of all for the sake of my daughter.

The brokenness, the imperfection—they're a gift, you see. Because, somehow, though it makes no sense at all, pain leads us deeper into whom we are meant to be.

Chapter 10

Y'ALL

His name was Aylan Kurdi. He was three years old. And, on September 2, 2015, his body washed up on the shore of a Turkish beach. A photo of his body lying lifeless on the beach appeared around the world in newspapers, online news sources, and television programs. It remains one of the most soul-shattering images I have ever seen. And, even as I wish I could forget the image, I wish, too, that we all, everyone of us in these United States, were required to have the photo framed over our dining room tables...our fireplace mantles...anywhere that we'd have to look at it every day and be conscious of what this world we live in is capable of—and what role we play in such horror.

Aylan was one of millions—millions—of refugees from the country of Syria. In the first four-and-a-half years of the war, since the Syrian civil war broke out in March of 2011, an estimated 9 million Syrians have fled their homes.

Fled their homes.

I cannot fathom having to grab up Maddy, jam all that we could into our backpacks, and leave. Just leave. Walking, hitchhiking, relying on total strangers for food and shelter at times—things I could never imagine us doing. Even if it meant risking death because the alternative—staying put—meant certain death. I

cannot fathom. But exactly that is happening all over the world we live in—in Rwanda, in Myanmar, in Uganda, in Syria. Most days, it is easy to turn a blind eye, to ignore the reality of it because it does not affect us.

But when the bodies of toddlers wash up on foreign shores because that beautiful boy's parents believed it safer to risk the sea than stay in their native land...the horror is impossible to ignore.

Aylan Kurdi. May we write his precious name on our hearts and, in doing so, refuse to settle for a world in which little boys die in the way he died.

☙ ❧

My colleague and friend Jim spent a great deal of his many years in ministry working with youth, leading conferences or mission trips—where there were many, many teenagers to lead, protect, and care for. On the first night of these gatherings, Jim would call together the adults involved in the event or trip, and he would remind them every child there was the responsibility of every adult there. "Your kids are my kids and my kids are your kids," he would say, and the adults would repeat back, "Your kids are my kids and my kids are your kids." It was both mandate and reminder that they were all in this together. That they were all "*their* kids."

I have often wondered what the world would be like if Jim's youth event words were something we lived every day.

Several months ago, a thirteen-year-old boy was shot in one of Louisville's more troubled and poverty-stricken neighborhoods. In the last year, someone's been shot every couple of days in Louisville. And there doesn't seem to be an end in sight to this rise in crime for my city. This eats at my soul.

Two particular things about this particular boy make the soul-eating worse. One is that it was a kid—a boy who could have been one of any boys in any one of my youth groups. Children die at the hands

of violence every day in this country. I get that. And, so—on the one hand—so what? Probably in other cities three times as many teenage boys have been shot.

"So what?" makes me crazy, because any child's harm or death, for whatever reason, is a cause for mourning. But when we've got middle-school-aged boys wielding firearms in our city streets, we ought to be falling to our knees, begging forgiveness for what we've become as a nation.

The other thing that really got to me about this particular boy is that, while I heard people acknowledge his shooting as a tragedy, I also heard far too much, "Ah. There goes that West End, being troublesome again." In Louisville, "West End" means "west of 9th Street." Ninth Street marks a significant socioeconomic and cultural divide in the city. Some might even say 9th Street segregates the city. East of 9th Street is downtown tourism, funky neighborhoods with boutiques and bars and indie coffee shops, suburbs and shopping malls and a thriving local restaurant scene. West of 9th Street is low-income housing, city parks where no one wants to be after dark, a drug trade, and frequent gun violence. West of 9th Street is mostly African American. East of 9th Street is not. Somewhere along the way, in the city of Louisville, we've become comfortable chalking things up to "West End" problems instead of recognizing a West End problem is, in fact, a Louisville problem.

We are, after all, one city.

What if instead of being so quick to name the shooting of an eighth grader as a product of the West End's issues, we'd all broken our hearts open grieving the lost life? What if we'd claimed this child of God as our child, too, and felt the bullet that killed him pierce our own hearts, our own lives, our own little ones tucked safely in their beds?

What if Aylan's death brought constant, unabated grief into all of our lives, grief so palpable that we could not see past it, grief that

compelled us to swear to do something about it? The kid at school that smells odd and never is quite dressed adequately and inhales her lunch every day because it's the only meal she knows she's getting—what if we surround her with every ounce of tangible love and light we have available and promise her she doesn't have to walk alone anymore? What if we not only took sandwiches down to the homeless community under the bridge, but also books? And sub-zero sleeping bags? And what if we said, "Here. Please. It's for your child. Because, if our lives had not been cast as they have, it could easily be me and my child sitting where you are." And then what if we offered to come back, every weekend, and in doing so made this homeless family a part of our lives? Offered them relationship along with the well-intended sandwich and thermos of coffee?

What if your kids were my kids? And my kids were your kids? For real?

Several years ago, a local domestic violence prevention/advocacy organization presented a program on bullying for middle schoolers at my congregation. Their program was effective for a variety of reasons, but one thing stood out to me: "In almost every instance of bullying," they told the kids, "there is actually a third person, aside from the victim and the bully." You could see the puzzled looks on the kids' faces at this—"What are they talking about?"

Bystanders. They were talking about bystanders, the people who watch injustice, or harm, or violence or suffering or immense sorrow take place, and, even if they feel a tug at their heartstrings, don't do anything about it. Shake their heads and walk away, choose not to be involved in helping another in a time of pain. Bystanders, these folks told those kids, can make or break a situation in which someone is being bullied.

I know all about cyber-bullying. And text-bullying. And the subtle ways a bully can make life a living hell for his or her victim, such that it takes any supposed bystander a long time to even realize something is happening. Vast injustice happens right under our

noses and we do not even realize it. But far too often we simply choose the bliss of ignorance, of, "What can I possibly do to fix this?" And, so, we simply stand still. Is this what we want for our young people, a society of bystanders?

I worked for a couple of years for a nonprofit that served single parents completing college degrees. The vast majority of the participants in this program have known homelessness, or at least unstable housing. They'd lived in poverty, escaped abusive relationships, dealt with the effects of malnutrition on themselves and their children. Most of them were scrabbling their way out of hell by tooth and nail. They were some of the strongest men and women, and the most dedicated parents, I've ever known, and I stood in daily awe of their tenacity and hope when I worked with them.

The nonprofit held a major fundraising luncheon every year, and, one year, the speaker for that luncheon was Los Angeles–based author and attorney Carissa Phelps.[1] Ms. Phelps is a survivor of human sex trafficking, and, having survived, has dedicated herself to advocacy and legal aid for children and adolescents who have been sex-trafficking victims themselves. As part of the luncheon plan, I gave a tour of the nonprofit's facilities to a regular volunteer and potential donor. She was a middle-aged white woman, privileged, highly educated, truly concerned about our participants and how she could support them.

As I told her Ms. Phelps' story, and, as the words "*human trafficking*" came out of my mouth, her eyes widened, and one hand slowly rose to cover her own gaping mouth. She was (and rightfully so) horrified at the story I was telling her.

Finally she said, "What country?" I didn't understand her question and it must have been obvious, because she repeated it, adding, "What country was she trafficked in?"

---

[1] Carissa Phelps' story is told in her memoir *Runaway Girl* (New York: Viking, 2012).

I paused. Took a deep breath. And answered, quietly and simply, "This one."

Her silence was a deafening response.

This one. The United States, land of the free and home of the brave, bootstraps, manifest destiny, equality, all that. This one. Where human trafficking, primarily of women and girls, primarily for sex work, is a multi-million-dollar-a-year industry.

The Polaris Project, a U.S.–based NGO dedicated to fighting the national human-trafficking business, received, in 2014 alone, over 24,000 "signals" for help from their various advocacy and intervention networks and services. And those are only the cases that can be tracked.

Carissa Phelps is not the only one. Far from it. We know this. We have data to prove it. And yet, still, there are children—our children—in slavery in these United States.

Are we okay being bystanders to this?

("Your kids are my kids. And my kids are your kids.")

I know it's overwhelming. Believe me, there are days getting Maddy to school on time, in clean clothes, with her teeth brushed and having been fed breakfast is a small victory for me. I say that as a mother with resources, with support, with education, with ways and means. I need—need—the village of people raising my daughter. I need and am grateful for the full parental partnership of her dad, even as we are no longer married. I need the friends who pick her up from school or keep her on a snow day when my workload is just too much. I need the calm assurance of my parents that I can do this thing called motherhood, and the way my sister and brother-in-law treat Maddy as if she is their own, even though they live nowhere near us. I cannot do it alone.

And if my Maddy were in trouble, in harm's way, in danger—I'd want any bystander to step up and keep her safe. And I hope—

pray—I'd be brave and committed enough to do the same to another's child in need.

This caring for our children, it is not a competitive or solo sport. When we make it such, we fail them all. Every one. We must be in this together.

When Maddy was born, I served a congregation where I had a colleague named Mary Beth. When I arrived on that staff, just shy of age thirty-one and so terribly nervous about meeting new people and working with new youth, Mary Beth, who'd been on that church's staff as long as I'd been alive, took the time to show me the ropes. She walked me through the congregation's history, made sure I knew who was related to who, and gave me instructions for how to lead the communion service my first Sunday. When she was done with all that, she checked in on me on a regular basis.

I've never known anyone quite like Mary Beth. She was grizzled and tough and deeply caring. She could argue her point fiercely in a board meeting and an hour later sit quietly and compassionately at the bedside of someone ill, or in the living room of someone dealing with grief, or at a local dive with a cigarette in hand talking to just about anyone. She maneuvered the giant aging church bus as easily—and perhaps with as much pleasure—as she could her Porsche. She cared nothing for style or fashion of any kind, though she did once, before a major church event, call me to ask, "Are we (as in the two of us, the only women on staff) going with skirts or slacks for this shindig?"

Mary Beth had no biological children of her own, but she was, somehow, profoundly maternal. When Maddy was about six weeks old, I brought her to church for the first time—it was a Sunday evening youth fundraiser and fellowship dinner, and I was barely ready to be in public, my C-section incision site still painful at times and my energy very low. Maddy's dad and I walked into a full church fellowship hall, and I remember thinking, "I cannot do this. All these people. I'm so overwhelmed." Within moments,

Mary Beth was at my side. She took Maddy gently from me, cradled Maddy in her arms, and said, "I've got her." Mary Beth knew, with one look at me, that I needed a moment, that someone was going to have to help me navigate the situation. I was grateful—but nowhere near as grateful as I was for what Mary Beth did next.

With Maddy curled up quietly in her arms, Mary Beth walked from table to table, from person to person, saying, "This is Maddy. This is our new baby. Isn't she beautiful?" There has, I'm sure of it, never been a more intentional introduction of a child to a group of people.

This is *our* baby. That's what she said. And I wonder how different this world would be if such a thing were said about every child—if every single beautiful one of them was taken up into arms as kind and caring as Mary Beth's and claimed "ours."

Less than a year later, Mary Beth lay dying in a hospital bed. She'd defeated cancer before, and she was battling it again—but this time, she was losing. She was alert and attentive, but her days were numbered, and so, one by one, day after day, friends, family, and colleagues came to see her. And, one day, I took Maddy to see her. Mary Beth was awake, but so tired. All around her were beeping machines and tubes dripping medicine, but she smiled when she saw me walk in with Maddy in tow. Without even thinking about it, I carefully placed Maddy in the curve of Mary Beth's arm, and I said, "I thought she might do you some good." I will always remember the image of the two of them in that hospital bed, the very young and healthy, and the very sick and dying, together.

When I say, "We must be in this together," this is the image that comes to mind: Maddy and Mary Beth. In retrospect it feels like they shepherded one another through that year—Maddy's first and Mary Beth's last—in such a way that they were both better and stronger for it.

One of my favorite and most-oft used words is *y'all*. I often seen it misspelled (ya'll) and I often hear people make fun of it as a "Southern thing." It's an informal contraction of "you all," and technically, I guess, it can be used when speaking to one person or a group. That said, it is not uncommon in the South to have someone to say to you, just you alone, "How y'all doin' today?" To which I generally say, "Just fine, how're y'all?"

I use y'all often when speaking or preaching, and generally when I'm about to make a point—as in, "Y'all... (boom, mike drop, exit podium!)." And when I was doing youth ministry I often would holler to a big bunch of kids, "Y'all! Hey! Listen up!"

Sometimes you hear someone really stress the plural nature of "y'all" by saying, "All y'all!" As in, "All y'all are welcome!" Or, "All y'all need to listen up." In other words, "y'all" just won't quite cut it, so, to be clear, I mean every single one of you, "*All* y'all!"

I don't know what the first-person plural of "y'all" might be—not in the same sense anyway. "We all" just doesn't carry the same punch. "Y'all"—that makes a statement. It's indicates familiarity, gets people's attention. Truly, there isn't another word quite like it.

So...

Y'all, we need each other—you and me and everyone else. All y'all. Every single one. We must be in this together. For my kids and your kids. For all our kids.

CONCLUSION: CHOOSING HOPE

Last summer, just before school started, Maddy and I took a quick trip to North Carolina to visit my parents. They live on the eastern side of the state, a couple of hours from the coast, and as a summer's end treat, my mom made plans for us to visit Shackleford Island, a small island on North Carolina's Outer Banks—uninhabited and unsettled by human beings, and home to a herd of wild horses. The island is protected by the state park system, and there isn't so much as an outhouse, old wooden bench, or makeshift shelter of any kind for human beings. The island belongs to the horses.

The inner shore of the island faces the calmer inland waters that make up the bay of Beaufort, North Carolina. The outer shore is the Atlantic Ocean, and the day we visited, we landed a couple of hours before afternoon high tide. Across the island's sand dunes and scrub brush, you could already see the waves kicking up and the vast expanse of beach disappearing under the water's edge.

Whether or not you actually see the island's residents is pure luck. And we got very lucky. As we walked off the boat that had brought us across the bay and to the island, about six of the horses were already hanging out along the beach, one of them a newborn colt, just eight weeks old according to the crusty captain who'd gotten us across. "Be careful," he said, "They're wild animals. Pretty to look at, but not pets."

I repeated his cautionary words to Maddy, her eyes already as big as saucers, her flip-flops already kicked off, and her long legs already

dashing across the sand to get a closer look at the beautiful beasts.

And, truly, it was magical. The horses waded through shallow tide pools, stopping to nibble vegetation here and there, occasionally looking up at the dozen or so two-legged visitors madly snapping cameras in what seemed like quiet amusement. We humans were mostly silent. An unspoken agreement to disrupt the horses as little as possible seemed to have been made among us all, and if anyone did speak, it was in low, almost whispered tones.

After taking a few shots of my girl with the horses in the background, I asked if she wanted to go look for shells along the water. She readily agreed, and so she and I and my mom set off to do just that. Meanwhile, my dad had gone further into the island,

Maddy at Shackleford Island

across the first line of sand dunes, having seen another group of horses he wanted to get a closer look at. No one was in a hurry—we had two hours before the boat would be back for us.

As Mom and Maddy and I turned toward the water and our shell-seeking adventure, I looked up and noticed something that gave me pause—dark storm clouds rolling in from across the bay and Beaufort. Very dark ones. Moving quickly.

"Mom?" I said, and as she looked at me in response I simply pointed my finger toward the sky. Her gaze widened in realization of what I was indicating and I said, "There's nowhere to go."

And, five minutes later, when those clouds exploded in a fury of wind and rain, all of it intensified by the ocean's waters stirred up and angry themselves, there wasn't...anywhere to go.

"Mommy!" Maddy screamed and ran over to me. I turned my back to the rain and tried to shelter her little body as best I could. Mom scanned the horizon for my dad, any efforts to call his name futile.

"He's over there!" I hollered over the storm and directed her to a still figure in a broad-rimmed hat, hunkered down off in the distance behind a dune, his backpack keeping him propped up. And "over there" she went, wanting to be sure her husband was okay.

Maddy, meanwhile, was less than thrilled with the situation. The rain stung, and the wind was hard to stand up against for me, much less her. "Mommy, what will we do?" she wailed.

I thought fast. Made a decision. And, pulling her close to me, I said, "Maddy, we have two choices. I cannot get the boat here faster. And there is no shelter. And I know this is hard. So we can choose to be miserable." She nodded, clearly identifying with the word "*miserable*."

I soldiered on, "Or, we can choose to see this as an adventure. We can dance in this rain. And run and play in it. We're already wet. And if we choose adventure, for the rest of our lives, you and I will

be able to tell people about the day we got stuck in the rain with a bunch of wild horses on a deserted island."

I've never in my life been prouder of her than when she responded, a valiant effort at smiling beginning to make itself known across her face, "Okay, Mommy. Okay."

And so we danced. And ran. And skipped. And sang. And watched the horses huddle together against the storm. And kept an eye on Dad as best we could at our distance from him.

I don't know how long exactly the storm lasted, but I know it felt like it was going on for a very long time. Just as I thought maybe the storm was beginning to wane, Maddy exclaimed, "Mommy! There's Neana!" and across the top of the dunes I saw my Mom walking determinedly toward a tall thicket of brush. She saw us too, and waved us over, pointing toward the brush.

"Maddy," I said, "I think Neana has an idea," and sure enough, Neana did. For the last several minutes of that storm, Maddy and Mom and I huddled underneath a large bush of some sort, its strong branches and thick, wiry leaves enough to keep the worst of the wind and rain off of us.

The absurdity of it all struck me as the three of us crouched low under the branches. "Mom," I said, "Is this really happening?" and we both descended into laughter at ourselves. Here we were, in the year 2015, every gift of modernity normally at our disposal, but, in that moment on Shackleford Island, we were entirely defenseless against nature—completely at the mercy of the earth and its mighty ways.

And then, as the last bit of wind receded and a hint of sun peeked out from the thinning clouds, and the rain died down, Maddy exclaimed with all the joy of a child who has just experienced something amazing, "This is the Best. Day. *Ever!*"

And it was. We crawled out from under our sheltering bush, and saw Dad rising up from his protective dune and heading toward

us. And the horses shifted out of their huddle and the colt kicked up its heels and ran across the sand with such glee. And a gentle ocean breeze began to dry us out. And the tide rolled in and we found shells upon shells and drank in the beauty of how wild and unexpected and perfect it had all been.

Perfect because we chose to make it so. Not because things had gone as planned. Not because we were entirely comfortable (wet underclothes do not for happy people make). Not because hot showers were at our immediate disposal.

Not at all. Perfect because, in a crucial moment, we made a choice to give ourselves to what was happening and so salvage the joy to be found in simply being alive. In simply being together. In simply having been held safe in the midst of it all.

It was the best day ever because we chose to believe it had been.

I've written in these pages about experiences and people that have led me to hope. I've shared the things about being Maddy's mom that drive me to believe in a better world for her and her peers. I've offered some thoughts on what it means to learn from our children, trusting that they know things we don't.

I have, in many, many ways, had a very fortunate life. There are many who face much greater challenge and loss and heartache than the things I've told of in these pages. Not a one of us escapes life unscathed—in fact, at the core of living is a realization that it will not always be easy. Sometimes, this life threatens to destroy us. But, oh—oh the moments when it puts us back together again, when it calls us out of hurt and fear and into trust and love.

At the end of the day, and everything I've written in this book aside, I choose hope. Just like Maddy chose to make a stormy day at the beach her best day ever, I actively, consciously, intentionally, and despite any evidence of its existence to the contrary, I choose hope.

This is more difficult some days than others. As I was finishing the manuscript for this book, the world we live in was reeling from a series of terrorist attacks in Paris and in Beirut. The Middle East remains in turmoil. A nine-year-old boy was gunned down in broad daylight on the streets of Chicago. Over the summer a group of black men and women who had gathered for prayer at their church in Charleston, South Carolina, were murdered by a lone white gunman. Every day, it seems, as I wrote, another fearful story can be added, and I fear, deeply and daily, what Maddy's future might hold.

But still, I choose hope. I choose not to let the fear control me.

I know no other way to have being. Even on the days when I am terrified of what might become of us all. Even on the days when I feel so small and insignificant. Even when I am wracked by insecurity and self-doubt. Still, and always…eventually, I choose hope.

That day at Shackleford, I found a cache of what at first seemed to be flat stones. As I dug them out of the sand and brushed away the grit from their surface, I realized they were pieces of shells—tossed and worn and broken apart from their original whole by the ocean that delivered them to that shore, velvet-smooth at the edges and cool to the touch, even on a hot summer's afternoon.

I carried them home to Kentucky. I washed away the dirt and grime, and now they sit in my living room, in a pottery bowl on an old wooden table that used to belong to my grandmother. Sometimes I gather a few of them in the palm of my hand and marvel at their simple beauty. Faint lines of color run across their surfaces, and they reflect the light available in the room when it shines just so across that bowl. They are, now, talismans of hope. Physical reminders— sacraments, even—of what it means to choose, in this life we live, a way of being that trusts the inherent goodness of the universe.

Because, the truth is that, choose all we want, some days are not the Best Days Ever. Not even close. And I, in writing about choosing

hope, do not mean to suggest that we can will away bad days or terrible experiences or the heartache this life often hands us. I speak only from what my own life has taught me, and what I have been taught is that there will be very bad days—both for me, personally, and the world, collectively.

Not long ago, during a particularly difficult time in my life, a dear friend who knows a thing or two herself about particularly difficult times, taught me a new word: *sisu*. It's a Finnish word, and it doesn't translate well into English—the closest thing perhaps is the phrase "having guts."

It takes *sisu* to navigate the worst days. Or, as we'd say down in my beloved native South, pure grit.

I do not always succeed at such grit. I do not always manage to channel *sisu*. But for my beautiful, precious daughter's sake, I keep trying. Despite my own shortcomings and mistakes, despite everything in this broken and beautiful world that would urge me to do anything but choose hope, on my best days, I do it anyway.

And…when I cannot, when it all seems just too much to bear, I trust that others are hoping *for* me. In particular, I trust the promise of a trusted friend, a precious brother in ministry and in life, who taught me what it means to hope *for* another person, to stand with another in her deepest and darkest days and say, "You will get through this. All is not lost."

And, so, this is my prayer: That we will hope *for* and *with* our children. Standing with them always, into the darkest night and straight on again until a bright new morning comes.

They need us so much, y'all. And we need them. Because, in truth, the greatest hope we have available to us is each other—our children and ourselves—forging our way as best we can, towards a kinder and more whole world. *Together.*

Notes